THIS

MODERN-DAY WITCH
2023 WHEEL OF THE YEAR
PLANNER

BELONGS TO

_____

_____

_____

_____

The Modern-Day Witch

2023
WHEEL OF THE YEAR
17-MONTH PLANNER

SHAWN ROBBINS &
CHARITY BEDELL

STERLING ETHOS
New York

STERLING ETHOS
New York

STERLING ETHOS and the distinctive Sterling Ethos logo
are registered trademarks of Sterling Publishing Co., Inc.

ISBN 978-1-4549-4588-8

Distributed in Canada by Sterling Publishing Co., Inc., c/o Canadian Manda Group, 664 Annette Street, Toronto, Ontario, Canada M6S 2C8. Distributed in the United Kingdom by GMC Distribution Services, Castle Place, 166 High Street, Lewes, East Sussex, England BN7 1XU. Distributed in Australia by NewSouth Books, University of New South Wales, Sydney, NSW 2052, Australia

For information about custom editions, special sales, and premium and corporate purchases, please contact Sterling Special Sales at specialsales@sterlingpublishing.com.

Printed in Malaysia

2 4 6 8 10 9 7 5 3

sterlingpublishing.com

Interior design by Jordan Wannemacher and Elizabeth Mihaltse Lindy
Cover design by Jordan Wannemacher

PICTURE CREDITS – See page 191

Contents

Introduction

This planner is filled with spells, recipes, and lore to help you live your best life. Today's witches follow a modern festival calendar loosely based on ancient festivals from Norse and Celtic traditions. While the monthly moon celebrations are the primary time for major spell workings, each Sabbat provides a unique opportunity to work magic and experience the mysteries.

THE WICCAN CYCLE

The story of the Lord and Lady (or Sun God and Goddess) of modern Wicca, based on ancient fertility myths, explains the cycle of birth, growth, life, death, decay, and finally rebirth, the same cycle you can observe in nature every year. There is really no transition from one form to another as time flows on. The cycle follows the calendar year; traditionally the Wheel starts with Yule (the winter solstice), but to follow the cycle of the story linearly, we will start with Imbolc.

Imbolc happens in early February, when the young Sun God is born. It is a time to plan and prepare for the next season. Seeds and farming tools are blessed for the planting season. Then we have Ostara (spring equinox), when the Goddess becomes both a maiden and a mother, and the God a small boy. Innocence

and rebirth are the themes. Spring has begun. It is a time for a fresh start and new projects. Beltane is the next holiday. Here, the God has reached maturity and the God and Goddess marry each other. It is a day of honoring fertility in all its forms. Couples jumped over broomsticks to ensure the fertility of the land. Litha (summer solstice) follows, where we celebrate the strength and power of the young God. The land is fertile and full of life. The God has just reached the height of his virility.

Lughnasadh/Lammas comes after, the first of the harvest festivals. We honor the year's first bounty through feasts, games, and bonfires. Mabon (autumnal equinox) is the second harvest festival. Here the Sun God is sacrificed for the good of the land. His death means future harvests, fertile herds, and bountiful crops for the next season. Samhain is the final harvest and the night witches welcome and honor the return of the dead. The God is in the underworld, starting his process to be reborn in the spring. Finally, there is Yule, the return of the sun. The God's journey through the underworld is done and his journey to be reborn to the land is just beginning.

May you find this information useful and may your path be blessed.

WHEEL OF THE YEAR

The Wheel of the Year is a modern myth that tells the story of the life cycle of the Lord and Lady of modern Wicca (see pages 4–5). All life is connected through this cycle, which is celebrated through the festivals and Sabbats that occur during the Wheel of the Year. The solstice and equinox descriptions here correspond to the Northern Hemisphere; in the Southern Hemisphere, the solstices and equinoxes are opposite; for example, Yule in the Southern Hemisphere is the longest day of the year.

As noted on page 4, the Wheel of the Year typically begins at Yule, the winter solstice, which can range from December 20–22, depending on the year. This planner begins in August 2022 and runs through December 2023, providing five additional months for planning and tracking both important festivals and everyday tasks and rituals. Each month starts off with a full monthly view calendar to give you an overview of key days for that month. (Note: Moon phases are set in Eastern Standard and adjusted for Daylight Saving Time.)

Yule (Winter Solstice) • December 20–23

Celebrates the shortest and darkest day of the year, which ranges yearly from December 20–23. This holiday, also known as Midwinter, corresponds with the Druid Alban Arthan (the Light of Arthur), and Christmas.

MAGICKAL WORK: Cinnamon broom of prosperity and protection

BASE RITUAL: Decorating Yule trees, staying up until sunrise to greet the new sun; decorating trees indoors and out is a common way to honor this Sabbat; making wreaths from evergreens also ensures prosperity for the land, and your home.

Imbolc • February 2

Imbolc, which translates from Old Irish as "in the belly," is an important feast day in the Celtic tradition. It marks the midway point between the winter solstice and the spring equinox. Also known as Saint Brigid's Day, it corresponds with Groundhog Day in the United States and Canada.

MAGICKAL WORK: Cleansing and blessing, witch's spring cleaning

BASE RITUAL: Light a single candle in a cauldron, then slowly light several other candles, to resemble returning light (maidens wearing candle wreaths is common in some traditions).

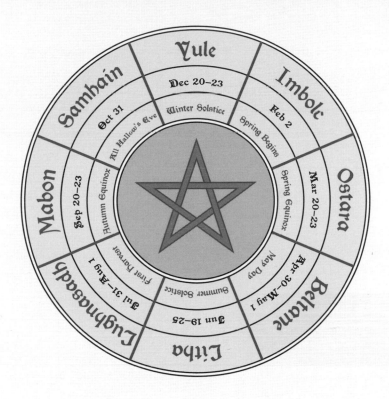

Ostara (Spring Equinox) • March 20–23

Ostara is celebrated on the spring, or vernal, equinox when the sun is directly above the equator; day and night are almost equal, heralding that spring is near (in the Northern Hemisphere). The name *Ostara* is derived from the Germanic goddess Eostre—from which Easter gets is name—goddess of the dawn, spring, and fertility.

MAGICKAL WORK: Sowing the seeds of success

BASE RITUAL: Dyeing and eating colored eggs, which represent the potential within each and every one of us

Beltane • April 30–May 1

Beltane is an ancient Gaelic fire festival, celebrated halfway between the spring and summer solstices. It is a time of bonfires, flowers, and dancing around maypoles—hence the corresponding holiday May Day—to welcome the coming warmth of spring, new life, and fertility.

MAGICKAL WORK: Fertility wand or maypole

BASE RITUAL: Great Rite; cows were directed between the bonfires to be blessed; couples made love in the fields to ensure fertile crops.

Litha (Summer Solstice) • June 19–25

Litha, also known as Midsummer, honors the summer solstice, the longest day the year, when the sun is at its peak. The holiday is typically celebrated from June 19–25, depending on the year.

MAGICKAL WORK: Dandelion wish spell

BASE RITUAL: Staying up all night greeting the morning with bonfires, telling stories and enjoying the length of the nights is part of this festival.

Lammas/Lughnasadh • July 31 (sundown)–August 1

Lammas or Lughnasadh, also known as Pagan Thanksgiving, falls almost halfway between the summer solstice and autumnal equinox. It is the first of three harvest Sabbats; celebrating fruits and grains, and is normally celebrated with a feast of thanks.

MAGICKAL WORK: Baking blessed bread

BASE RITUAL: Honors the first harvest and the first sacrifices of the land; host a family barbecue and relish life before winter sets in.

Mabon (Autumnal Equinox) • September 20–23

Mabon—celebrated at the autumnal equinox, the midpoint between harvesting and sowing crops—is the second harvest Sabbat. It is a time to give thanks as well as reflect on the past year and look ahead to the next one.

MAGICKAL WORK: Thankfulness

BASE RITUAL: Witches' feast; Mabon is the second harvest festival and the blood festival, and a time for thanksgiving with large feasts; potluck dinners are great ways to get the community involved in the celebration

Samhain (All Hallow's Eve) • October 31

Samhain, or All Hallow's Eve, marked the third harvest before winter. It celebrates the circle of life by honoring those who have passed away, and corresponds with Halloween and the Day of the Dead.

MAGICKAL WORK: Warding against evil spirits; divinations

BASE RITUAL: Samhain is a time to honor the dead and our ancestors. Jack-o'-lanterns were used to ward off evil spirits as families traveled to be together to honor their ancestors; we have a Dumb Supper, where we set empty places at the table for our ancestors and offer them a bit of each item from the feast.

MAGICKAL MOON PHASES

By Leanna Greenaway

For thousands of years, the moon has been seen as having a magickal presence, and even our ancestors believed that it had some spiritual significance. There are numerous spells that you can perform during different phases of the moon—certain spells work better during particular phases. All the spells listed on pages 10–11 can be cast in a simple ritual: Take a small white candle to the window and gaze at the moon through the windowpane. Say your wish out loud and with feeling, then leave the candle to burn down (while you are still in the room, of course; do not leave the candle unattended or place it near a curtain).

New Moon ●

New Moons usually cannot be seen with the naked eye. But a day or two after the new moon first appears each month, a slim crescent moon becomes visible. The new moon phase surrounds us with lots of positive energy and can act as a catalyst for immediate change. Many transitions naturally happen around a new moon anyway, such as new jobs, births, and moves, but if you need to revolutionize your life, cast spells at this time for:

Career changes / Moving house swiftly and easily / Safe and enjoyable travel / Increasing your cash flow / Better health / Conceiving

Waxing Crescent ● to First Quarter Moon ☽

When the moon is waxing, witches like to cast spells for improving situations or for getting things going if things have been in a rut. Often, when life is unchanging, it takes a little boost to amp things up a bit, and this phase is definitely the best time to kick-start your life. This calendar only includes the first quarter moon symbol, not the waxing crescent. The first quarter moon symbol is shown on the days that the first quarter moon occurs. The waxing crescent phases occur between the new moon and the first quarter phases. The following spells act faster during a waxing moon:

Lifting one's mood / Getting out of a rut / Passing examinations and tests / Finding lost objects / Healing a sick animal or finding a lost pet / Nurturing abundant, healthy gardens and the well-being of nature / Losing weight or stopping smoking

Full Moon ○

From a magickal point of view the full moon does not have any negative connotations; it is just considered a very powerful time of the month. For some reason, Fridays that fall on full moons are wonderful days for casting love spells. There are lots of other spells that benefit from being cast on a full moon, too:

Protecting your home and property / Adding vigor to your life / Anything to do with love / Increasing self-confidence / Advancing in career and work / Enhancing psychic ability / Clairvoyance / Strengthening friendships and family bonds / Performing general good-luck spells

Waning Crescent ◑ to Last Quarter Moon ◐

The waning moon is the perfect time to cast spells for getting rid of the black clouds and negative energies that sometimes hang over us. This calendar only includes the last quarter moon symbol, not the waning crescent. The last quarter moon symbol is shown on the days that the last quarter moon occurs. The waning crescent phases occur between the last quarter and the new moon phases. It is a time when you can draw down strength from the universe. If you are surrounded by difficult people and feel you can't cope, or if you have to tackle difficult situations head-on, you can use the moon's power to assist you. By casting spells during this phase, you will gain the power to take control again, strengthen your weak areas, and become more assertive in your actions. Cast spells at this time for:

Developing inner strength and assertiveness / Banishing enemies /
Stopping arguments / Soothing unruly children / Calming anxiety /
Getting out of tricky situations

Dark or Void of the Moon

The dark moon, when the face of the moon is hidden, is also known as the "dead" moon. It takes place three days before a new moon and is considered to be the most magickal and potent of all the phases. Sadly, many people who practice black magick do so at this time. You might think that someone working on the darker side of the occult could not influence any spells or rituals that you might be performing, but the collective power mustered by these individuals can cause cosmic havoc: our spells may become confused or simply not work at all. It is a shame, because the brilliance and power of this phase is incredible, and without the negative manipulation I am sure we witches could do a great deal of good in it. Unless you are an experienced wand waver, it is probably best not to attempt any rituals at this time, but to wait until the new moon comes in.

17-MONTH
PLANNER

AUGUST 2022

Sunday	Monday	Tuesday	Wednesday
31	1	2	3
	Lammas/Lughnasadh (began at sundown, July 31)		
7	8	9	10
14	15	16	17
21	22	23	24
28	29	30	31
	Summer bank holiday (UK)		

Thursday	Friday	Saturday	NOTES
4	5	6	
	First Quarter Moon ◑		
11	12	13	
Full Moon ○			
18	19	20	
	Last Quarter Moon ◐		
25	26	27	
		New Moon ●	
1	2	3	

Lammas/Lughnasadh

By Connie Lavoie

Lughnasadh—also known as Lammas, Loafmas, Lúnasa, or Pagan Thanksgiving—is one of the four cross-quarter days between the solstices and equinoxes. . . . It is one of the four fire festivals and a Celtic holiday celebrated by many Wiccans and neo-pagans, especially those with roots in Celtic culture. Lughnasadh is the first Sabbat of the fruits and grains, as it happens when the grains and fruits from the year's first harvest are picked, so it is normally celebrated with a feast. Handfasting (Wiccan wedding) ceremonies are also often held during Lughnasadh. They say that some of our ancient ancestors would cut the first harvest corn and other grains and then go to the mountains and bury them as offerings to the gods for thanks and continued good harvests. People would come from miles around to trade, sell, and share their bounty and other goods. . . . There was dancing, plus drinking of ale, plenty of games, and tall tales to be told around the bonfires. . . . Today, we can still celebrate by giving thanks to the gods, the workers, and the spirits of the earth for these gifts and for the blessings of friends and family. We can invite our friends, families, coworkers, and neighbors for a potluck dinner of breads, cakes, fruits, and veggies and to sit around a bonfire and tell stories.

AUGUST 2022

1 MONDAY

Lammas/Lughnasadh (began at sundown, July 31)

2 TUESDAY

3 WEDNESDAY

4 THURSDAY

AUGUST 2022						
S	M	T	W	T	F	S
	1	2	3	4	5	6
7	8	9	10	11	12	13
14	15	16	17	18	19	20
21	22	23	24	25	26	27
28	29	30	31			

5 FRIDAY

First Quarter Moon ◑

SEPTEMBER 2022						
S	M	T	W	T	F	S
				1	2	3
4	5	6	7	8	9	10
11	12	13	14	15	16	17
18	19	20	21	22	23	24
25	26	27	28	29	30	

6 SATURDAY

7 SUNDAY

AUGUST 2022

8 MONDAY

9 TUESDAY

10 WEDNESDAY

11 THURSDAY

Full Moon ⚪

12 FRIDAY

AUGUST 2022						
S	M	T	W	T	F	S
	1	2	3	4	5	6
7	8	9	10	11	12	13
14	15	16	17	18	19	20
21	22	23	24	25	26	27
28	29	30	31			

SEPTEMBER 2022						
S	M	T	W	T	F	S
				1	2	3
4	5	6	7	8	9	10
11	12	13	14	15	16	17
18	19	20	21	22	23	24
25	26	27	28	29	30	

13 SATURDAY

14 SUNDAY

15 MONDAY

16 TUESDAY

17 WEDNESDAY

18 THURSDAY

AUGUST 2022						
S	M	T	W	T	F	S
	1	2	3	4	5	6
7	8	9	10	11	12	13
14	15	16	17	18	19	20
21	22	23	24	25	26	27
28	29	30	31			

19 FRIDAY

Last Quarter Moon ◑

SEPTEMBER 2022						
S	M	T	W	T	F	S
				1	2	3
4	5	6	7	8	9	0
11	12	13	14	15	16	17
18	19	20	21	22	23	24
25	26	27	28	29	30	

20 SATURDAY | **21** SUNDAY

Shawn Robbins's
After-Dinner Holiday Treat

This smoothie is delicious, fun to make, and good for your health. The dash of alcohol makes it a festive dessert treat for Lughnasadh (see page 16), when fresh berries are in season. (But you can have it on other holidays, too, and this recipe can be made with fresh or frozen fruit.)

Serves 2 to 3

Ingredients

½ cup (100 g) strawberries

½ cup (50 g) blueberries

½ cup (65 g) raspberries

1 banana

1 cup (250 g) flavored yogurt (any flavor you like)

1 tablespoon vanilla

½ cup (120 ml) pineapple juice

8 ice cubes

MAGICKAL INGREDIENT: A shot of your favorite fruit-flavored liquor, for added sweetness (I recommend cherry vodka).

Place all of the ingredients in a blender, and blend on high until the mixture is smooth. Drink up and enjoy.

22 MONDAY

---

23 TUESDAY

---

24 WEDNESDAY

---

25 THURSDAY

---

26 FRIDAY

---

27 SATURDAY | **28** SUNDAY

New Moon

AUGUST/SEPTEMBER 2022

29 MONDAY

Summer bank holiday (UK)

30 TUESDAY

31 WEDNESDAY

1 THURSDAY

2 FRIDAY

3 SATURDAY   **4** SUNDAY

First Quarter Moon ◗

Sunday	Monday	Tuesday	Wednesday
28	29	30	31
4	5 Labor Day (US, CAN)	6	7
11	12	13	14
18	19	20	21
25 Rosh Hashanah (begins at sundown) New Moon ●	26	27	28

Thursday	Friday	Saturday
1	2	3
8	9	10 Full Moon ◯
15	16	17 Last Quarter Moon ◑
22 Mabon (Autumnal Equinox)	23	24
29	30	1

SEPTEMBER 2022

5 MONDAY

Labor Day (US, CAN)

6 TUESDAY

7 WEDNESDAY

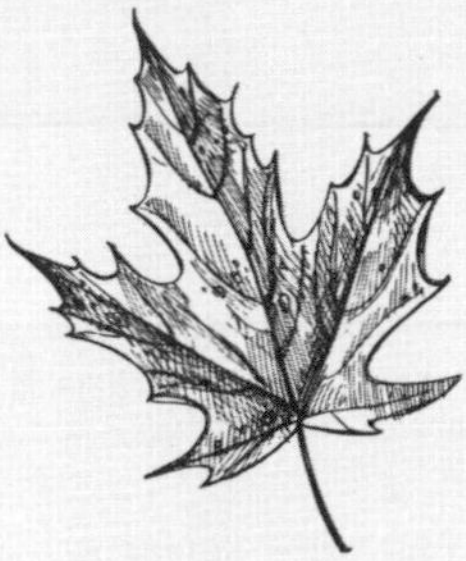

8 THURSDAY

9 FRIDAY

10 SATURDAY

Full Moon ◯

11 SUNDAY

SEPTEMBER 2022

12 MONDAY

13 TUESDAY

14 WEDNESDAY

15 THURSDAY

SEPTEMBER 2022

S	M	T	W	T	F	S
				1	2	3
4	5	6	7	8	9	10
11	12	13	14	15	16	17
18	19	20	21	22	23	24
25	26	27	28	29	30	

16 FRIDAY

OCTOBER 2022

S	M	T	W	T	F	S
						1
2	3	4	5	6	7	8
9	10	11	12	13	14	15
16	17	18	19	20	21	22
23	24	25	26	27	28	29
30	31					

17 SATURDAY

18 SUNDAY

Last Quarter Moon ◑

SEPTEMBER 2022

19 MONDAY

20 TUESDAY

21 WEDNESDAY

22 THURSDAY

Mabon (Autumnal Equinox)

23 FRIDAY

SEPTEMBER 2022						
S	M	T	W	T	F	S
				1	2	3
4	5	6	7	8	9	10
11	12	13	14	15	16	17
18	19	20	21	22	23	24
25	26	27	28	29	30	

OCTOBER 2022						
S	M	T	W	T	F	S
						1
2	3	4	5	6	7	8
9	10	11	12	13	14	15
16	17	18	19	20	21	22
23	24	25	26	27	28	29
30	31					

24 SATURDAY

25 SUNDAY

Rosh Hashanah
(begins at sundown)

New Moon

Magick by Essential Oils

Essential oils can be used individually in spells or rituals. In casting a love spell, you could anoint yourself with rose or patchouli oil to attract love and bring sensual energy to the situation. If you are having a hard time meditating, you could apply a few drops of frankincense or myrrh oil to your forehead and temples (although do a patch test first to make sure you have no allergies). If you are trying to attract money, a bit of ginger oil on a green candle could do the trick. The following list provides some of the most common essential oils and the attributes and areas that they correspond to when used in spells.

CHAMOMILE: Sleep, dreams, meditation, peace, money

CINNAMON: Physical energy, psychic awareness, prosperity

FRANKINCENSE: Spirituality, meditation

GINGER: Magickal energy, igniting sexual passion, love, money, courage

LAVENDER: Health, love, celibacy, conscious mind

LEMON: Health, purification

MUGWORT: Psychic awareness, psychic dreams, astral projection, spirituality

MYRRH: Spirituality, meditation, healing

PATCHOULI: Igniting sexual passion, love, fertility, money, jinx breaking

PEPPERMINT: Aid in meditation and trance work, purification, focus

ROSE: Igniting sexual passion, love, romance, peace, beauty

ROSEMARY: Longevity, memory, love, aid in meditation and trance work

SANDALWOOD: Spirituality, meditation, igniting sexual passion, healing

TEA TREE: Strength; cleansing; wards off unwanted spiritual attention, negativity, hexes, and curses; healing; protection

SEPTEMBER/OCTOBER 2022

26 MONDAY

27 TUESDAY

28 WEDNESDAY

29 THURSDAY

30 FRIDAY

1 SATURDAY

2 SUNDAY

First Quarter Moon ◐

OCTOBER 2022

Sunday	Monday	Tuesday	Wednesday
25	26	27	28
2 First Quarter Moon ◑	3	4 Yom Kippur (begins at sundown)	5
9 Full Moon ◯	10 Indigenous Peoples' Day, Columbus Day (US), Thanksgiving (CAN)	11	12
16	17 Last Quarter Moon ◐	18	19
23	24	25 New Moon ●	26
30	31 Samhain, Halloween	1	2

Thursday	Friday	Saturday
29	30	1
6	7	8
13	14	15
20	21	22
27	28	29
3	4	5

NOTES

OCTOBER 2022

3 MONDAY

---

4 TUESDAY

Yom Kippur (begins at sundown)

---

5 WEDNESDAY

---

6 THURSDAY

OCTOBER 2022

S	M	T	W	T	F	S
						1
2	3	4	5	6	7	8
9	10	11	12	13	14	15
16	17	18	19	20	21	22
23	24	25	26	27	28	29
30	31					

7 FRIDAY

NOVEMBER 2022

S	M	T	W	T	F	S
		1	2	3	4	5
6	7	8	9	10	11	12
13	14	15	16	17	18	19
20	21	22	23	24	25	26
27	28	29	30			

8 SATURDAY

9 SUNDAY

Full Moon ○

10 MONDAY

Indigenous Peoples' Day,
Columbus Day (US),
Thanksgiving (CAN)

11 TUESDAY

12 WEDNESDAY

13 THURSDAY

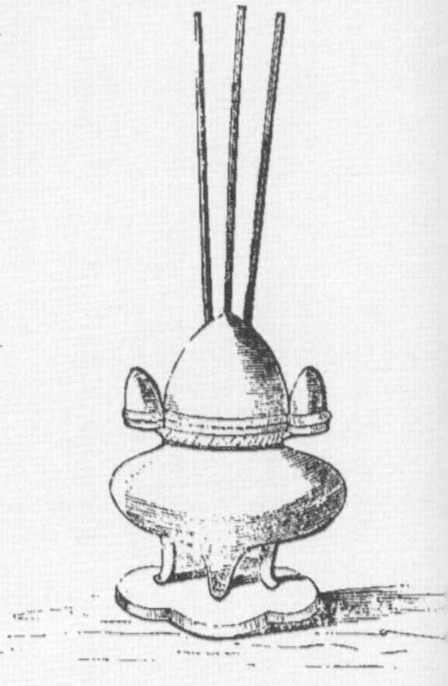

14 FRIDAY

15 SATURDAY

16 SUNDAY

OCTOBER 2022

17 MONDAY

Last Quarter Moon ◑

_____

18 TUESDAY

_____

19 WEDNESDAY

_____

20 THURSDAY

OCTOBER 2022						
S	M	T	W	T	F	S
						1
2	3	4	5	6	7	8
9	10	11	12	13	14	15
16	17	18	19	20	21	22
23	24	25	26	27	28	29
30	31					

21 FRIDAY

NOVEMBER 2022						
S	M	T	W	T	F	S
		1	2	3	4	5
6	7	8	9	10	11	12
13	14	15	16	17	18	19
20	21	22	23	24	25	26
27	28	29	30			

22 SATURDAY | **23** SUNDAY

24 MONDAY

25 TUESDAY

New Moon ●

26 WEDNESDAY

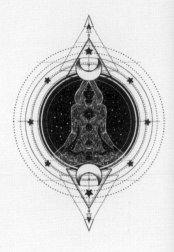

27 THURSDAY

28 FRIDAY

OCTOBER 2022						
S	M	T	W	T	F	S
						1
2	3	4	5	6	7	8
9	10	11	12	13	14	15
16	17	18	19	20	21	22
23	24	25	26	27	28	29
30	31					

29 SATURDAY

30 SUNDAY

NOVEMBER 2022						
S	M	T	W	T	F	S
		1	2	3	4	5
6	7	8	9	10	11	12
13	14	15	16	17	18	19
20	21	22	23	24	25	26
27	28	29	30			

Keep the Wildlife Healthy and Well

Witches often cast spells to encourage good health and well-being not only for themselves and their families, but also for all the living creatures in our environment. We feel it is important to try our best to keep every living thing happy and healthy. If you would like to magickally participate in helping your environment and protecting wildlife from illness and disease, try this spell.

Take a walk in the woods and collect a large bag of acorns. Acorns are considered to hold the properties of protection and good fortune, and in numbers of twenty or more will produce a powerful barrier to ward off negativity. If you cannot find them, it's quite all right to source them online.

Take a few small twigs and fallen leaves from the ground to represent nature. Place all these woodland treasures into a drawstring bag. When you're back at home, set up your altar as follows: Scatter some sea salt on the altar surface to purify the space. Then place three green candles in the center and light them. Situate the pouch in front of the candles and say these words:

"Spirits of nature, the magick you weave,
Bring power to this spell with these acorns and leaves,
All of the creatures are healthy and free,
Bring total protection to all that we see."

Let the candles burn all the way down, and then gather up the salt and place it inside the pouch. On the next full moon, return to the woodland where you gathered your items and scatter them back on the ground. This magick will ensure that everything stays in balance. The animals will remain healthy and be protected forever.

NOVEMBER 2022

Sunday	Monday	Tuesday	Wednesday
30	31	1	2
		First Quarter Moon ◑	
6	7	8	9
Daylight Saving Time Ends (US, CAN)		Election Day (US) Full Moon ○	
13	14	15	16
			Last Quarter Moon ◐
20	21	22	23
			New Moon ●
27	28	29	30

	Thursday	Friday	Saturday	NOTES
	3	4	5	
	10	11	12	
		Veterans Day (US)		
	17	18	19	
	24	25	26	
	Thanksgiving (US)			
	1	2	3	

SAMHAIN
(ALL HALLOW'S EVE, OR HALLOWEEN)

By Melodie Starr Ball

Samhain, or All Hallow's Eve, marks the third harvest before winter. It corresponds with Halloween and the Day of the Dead. Halloween is one of the most magickal nights of the year! It is the night when a witch's power is strongest and when the veil between this world and the other side is thinnest. One of the original reasons for Halloween was, among other things, to celebrate the circle of life by honoring those who have passed away. On Halloween, we invite our dead ancestors to celebrate their lives with us and have a feast with candles, games, and sweets (Halloween parties). Some traditional food for a Halloween feast includes apples, pears, pumpkin pie, corn, cider, and meat. There is a tradition of burning hazel or pine incense and white sage to keep any negative spirits from entering your home. Many people hold séances because it is much easier to make contact with the other side at this time.

With a witch's powers spiking on this night, it is a good time to perform divination rituals. Whether you use tarot, water scrying, or another type of divination, any spell or ritual performed on Halloween night is sure to be a great success! Many people have bonfires on Halloween night. Some say this is to keep ghosts and goblins away; however, fire scrying, or divining the future by gazing into open flames, is another form of divination that is very effective.

OCTOBER/NOVEMBER 2022

31 MONDAY

Samhain, Halloween

1 TUESDAY

First Quarter Moon ◗

2 WEDNESDAY

3 THURSDAY

OCTOBER 2022						
S	M	T	W	T	F	S
						1
2	3	4	5	6	7	8
9	10	11	12	13	14	15
16	17	18	19	20	21	22
23	24	25	26	27	28	29
30	31					

4 FRIDAY

NOVEMBER 2022						
S	M	T	W	T	F	S
		1	2	3	4	5
6	7	8	9	10	11	12
13	14	15	16	17	18	19
20	21	22	23	24	25	26
27	28	29	30			

5 SATURDAY

6 SUNDAY

Daylight Saving Time Ends
(US, CAN)

7 MONDAY

---

8 TUESDAY

Election Day (US)

Full Moon ○

---

9 WEDNESDAY

---

10 THURSDAY

---

11 FRIDAY

---

12 SATURDAY | **13** SUNDAY

NOVEMBER 2022

14 MONDAY

15 TUESDAY

16 WEDNESDAY

Last Quarter Moon ◑

17 THURSDAY

NOVEMBER 2022						
S	M	T	W	T	F	S
		1	2	3	4	5
6	7	8	9	10	11	12
13	14	15	16	17	18	19
20	21	22	23	24	25	26
27	28	29	30			

18 FRIDAY

DECEMBER 2022						
S	M	T	W	T	F	S
				1	2	3
4	5	6	7	8	9	10
11	12	13	14	15	16	17
18	19	20	21	22	23	24
25	26	27	28	29	30	31

19 SATURDAY

20 SUNDAY

NOVEMBER 2022

21 MONDAY

22 TUESDAY

23 WEDNESDAY

New Moon ●

24 THURSDAY

Thanksgiving (US)

25 FRIDAY

26 SATURDAY

27 SUNDAY

28 MONDAY

29 TUESDAY

30 WEDNESDAY

First Quarter Moon ◗

1 THURSDAY

2 FRIDAY

3 SATURDAY

4 SUNDAY

NOVEMBER 2022						
S	M	T	W	T	F	S
		1	2	3	4	5
6	7	8	9	10	11	12
13	14	15	16	17	18	19
20	21	22	23	24	25	26
27	28	29	30			

DECEMBER 2022						
S	M	T	W	T	F	S
				1	2	3
4	5	6	7	8	9	10
11	12	13	14	15	16	17
18	19	20	21	22	23	24
25	26	27	28	29	30	31

Black-Salt Protection for the Home

This spell will help to protect your home from negative energy of all kinds, within and without.

Materials

- 2–3 charcoal discs (the small discs used to burn incense work well)
- Mortar and pestle
- 2 cups (550 g) sea salt
- ½ cup (approximately 20 leaves) white sage
- ¼ cup (or one large root) galangal root, chopped
- ¼ cup (25 g) bearberries (*Arctostaphylos uva-ursi*)*
- 2 tablespoons black peppercorns

Ritual

Place the charcoal in the mortar and grind it with the pestle. If it is too hard, add a little water. This will soften the charcoal, making it easier to grind.

Add the other ingredients and thoroughly grind everything into a powder that resembles black salt. Sprinkle the mixture first on all your windowsills and then around the base of your doorways while visualizing a large shield over your home.

Also scatter it into each corner of every room in your home. Feel the house being protected by an energetic field. As you go, say this spell in each room:

> *"Protection comes this way,*
> *All negativity banished this day."*

Repeat once a month, sweeping up the previous batch of salt before resetting a new batch.

*Available online

DECEMBER 2022

Sunday	Monday	Tuesday	Wednesday
27	28	29	30
4	5	6	7 Full Moon ◯
11	12	13	14
18	19	20	21 Yule (Winter Solstice)
25 Christmas Day	26 Kwanzaa, Boxing Day (CAN)	27 Christmas Day (substitute day, UK)	28

Thursday	Friday	Saturday
1	2	3
8	9	10
15	16	17
	Last Quarter Moon ◑	
22	23	24
	New Moon ●	
29	30	31
First Quarter Moon ◐		

5 MONDAY

6 TUESDAY

7 WEDNESDAY

Full Moon ○

8 THURSDAY

9 FRIDAY

10 SATURDAY | **11** SUNDAY

DECEMBER 2022

12 MONDAY

13 TUESDAY

14 WEDNESDAY

15 THURSDAY

DECEMBER 2022

S	M	T	W	T	F	S
				1	2	3
4	5	6	7	8	9	10
11	12	13	14	15	16	17
18	19	20	21	22	23	24
25	26	27	28	29	30	31

16 FRIDAY

Last Quarter Moon ◗

JANUARY 2023

S	M	T	W	T	F	S
1	2	3	4	5	6	7
8	9	10	11	12	13	14
15	16	17	18	19	20	21
22	23	24	25	26	27	28
29	30	31				

17 SATURDAY

18 SUNDAY

19 MONDAY

20 TUESDAY

21 WEDNESDAY

Yule (Winter Solstice)

22 THURSDAY

23 FRIDAY

New Moon ●

24 SATURDAY

25 SUNDAY

Christmas Day

Yule

By Derrie P. Carpenter

Yule is the pagan version of Christmas, and it is also the recognition of the winter solstice. It is a festive time to light your home with candles, as this Sabbat is also a fire Sabbat because it marks the rebirth of the sun.

Yule can be celebrated many different ways. The most common way is with a Yule log. Each species of tree is imbued with different magickal and spiritual properties. You can choose the type of wood that is right for you and your family: oak for strength, aspen for protection and spirituality, birch for fertility, pine for purification and prosperity. Before the Yule log is burned, it is decorated and displayed, often as a beautiful centerpiece for a holiday meal. Decorations may include candles, mistletoe, holly, cranberries, and cloth or paper ribbon.

THE YULE LOG

Healing Light Spell

Sometimes we want to try to heal the world and offer peace and hope. This spell can help us send light, love, hope, and healing to the world at large.

Materials

Sharp knife
Pink candle
2 teaspoons dried lavender

2 teaspoons dried catnip
2 teaspoons dried ginkgo leaf
World map

Ritual

Use the knife to inscribe the words *Love, Peace, and Light* on the candle. Mix the lavender, catnip, and ginkgo leaf together. Lay the world map across your altar or work surface. Sprinkle the herbal mixture across the map (be sure that a little bit of the powder lands on every continent). Light the pink candle and place it on the center of the map. As the candle burns, envision a pink light enveloping the earth. Recite the chant:

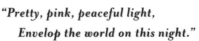

> *"Pretty, pink, peaceful light,*
> *Envelop the world on this night."*

Let the candle burn down (do not leave it unattended). Once the candle's burned completely, bury its remains and the herbs at a crossroads to send light and peace into the earth and through the earth to all of humanity.

DECEMBER 2022/JANUARY 2023

26 MONDAY

Kwanzaa
Boxing Day (CAN)

27 TUESDAY

Christmas Day (substitute day, UK)

28 WEDNESDAY

29 THURSDAY

First Quarter Moon ◐

30 FRIDAY

DECEMBER 2022						
S	M	T	W	T	F	S
				1	2	3
4	5	6	7	8	9	10
11	12	13	14	15	16	17
18	19	20	21	22	23	24
25	26	27	28	29	30	31

JANUARY 2023						
S	M	T	W	T	F	S
1	2	3	4	5	6	7
8	9	10	11	12	13	14
15	16	17	18	19	20	21
22	23	24	25	26	27	28
29	30	31				

31 SATURDAY

1 SUNDAY

New Year's Day

JANUARY 2023

Sunday	Monday	Tuesday	Wednesday
1 New Year's Day	2 Bank holiday (UK, CAN)	3	4
8	9	10	11
15	16 Martin Luther King Jr. Day	17	18
22 Lunar New Year (Year of the Rabbit)	23	24	25
29	30	31	1

Thursday	Friday	Saturday
5	6	7
	Full Moon ◯	
12	13	14
		Last Quarter Moon ◑
19	20	21
		New Moon ●
26	27	28
Australia Day		First Quarter Moon ◐
2	3	4

JANUARY 2023

2 MONDAY

Bank holiday (UK, CAN)

3 TUESDAY

4 WEDNESDAY

5 THURSDAY

JANUARY 2023						
S	M	T	W	T	F	S
1	2	3	4	5	6	7
8	9	10	11	12	13	14
15	16	17	18	19	20	21
22	23	24	25	26	27	28
29	30	31				

6 FRIDAY

Full Moon ◯

FEBRUARY 2023						
S	M	T	W	T	F	S
			1	2	3	4
5	6	7	8	9	10	11
12	13	14	15	16	17	18
19	20	21	22	23	24	25
26	27	28				

7 SATURDAY

8 SUNDAY

9 MONDAY

---

10 TUESDAY

---

11 WEDNESDAY

---

12 THURSDAY

---

13 FRIDAY

---

14 SATURDAY

Last Quarter Moon ◑

15 SUNDAY

JANUARY 2023

16 MONDAY

Martin Luther King Jr. Day

17 TUESDAY

18 WEDNESDAY

19 THURSDAY

JANUARY 2023						
S	M	T	W	T	F	S
1	2	3	4	5	6	7
8	9	10	11	12	13	14
15	16	17	18	19	20	21
22	23	24	25	26	27	28
29	30	31				

20 FRIDAY

FEBRUARY 2023						
S	M	T	W	T	F	S
			1	2	3	4
5	6	7	8	9	10	11
12	13	14	15	16	17	18
19	20	21	22	23	24	25
26	27	28				

21 SATURDAY

New Moon ●

22 SUNDAY

Lunar New Year
(Year of the Rabbit)

23 MONDAY

---

24 TUESDAY

---

25 WEDNESDAY

---

26 THURSDAY

Australia Day

---

27 FRIDAY

JANUARY 2023						
S	M	T	W	T	F	S
1	2	3	4	5	6	7
8	9	10	11	12	13	14
15	16	17	18	19	20	21
22	23	24	25	26	27	28
29	30	31				

---

28 SATURDAY

29 SUNDAY

First Quarter Moon ◗

FEBRUARY 2023						
S	M	T	W	T	F	S
			1	2	3	4
5	6	7	8	9	10	11
12	13	14	15	16	17	18
19	20	21	22	23	24	25
26	27	28				

A General Spell for Better Health

During the dark, freezing-cold days of winter, many people feel run-down and can become more susceptible to colds or flu. This spell can be used and adapted to keep you feeling strong and healthy in the winter or to simply keep you in great shape all year round.

MATERIALS

A yellow candle

1 tablespoon vegetable oil

9 drops basil oil

Candle holder

Sea salt, as needed

RITUAL

Prepare the candle by inscribing it with your name and the words "good health."

Blend the vegetable oil and basil oil, to promote vigor. Anoint the candle with this oil and place it in the candle holder.

Sprinkle salt around the base of the holder and light the candle. Say this spell three times:

"Surround my being in positive rays,
Encompass me and bless my being,
Shower healing light so that I might
Stay fit and well in the coming days."

Let the candle burn down (make sure not to leave it unattended) and repeat the spell once a month to ensure overall good health.

IMBOLC

By Rachel McGirr

Imbolc is an important feast day in the Celtic tradition, marking the midway point between the winter solstice and the spring equinox. It's a time of rebirth and hope that begins to stir in the long-awaited return of spring. In Ireland, where it's also known as Oimelc, celebratory Gaelic festivals are held all over the country from sunrise to sunset. Corn dollies, Brigid crosses, and corn cakes are made from the grains, reeds of straw, and wheat that were gathered at the harvest. The name "Imbolc" comes from the Old Irish *imblog*, which translates as "in the belly"—a reference to pregnant ewes and milking. Imbolc rituals took place in order to harness the divine energy that would help farmers grow a good supply of produce until the next harvest.

Imbolc Cake

You can prepare and bake this cake all in one baking tin!

Ingredients

1 2/3 cups (210 g) all-purpose flour	¼ cup (60 ml) vegetable oil
½ cup (100 g) sugar	1 tablespoon lemon peel
2 tablespoons poppy seeds	1 tablespoon orange peel
1 tablespoon baking soda	2 tablespoons lemon juice
½ tablespoon salt	2 tablespoons orange juice
¾ cup (180 ml) water	Powdered sugar

Preheat oven to 350°F (175°C). Mix flour, sugar, poppy seeds, baking soda, and salt with a fork in an ungreased 9 × 9 × 2-inch (23 × 23 × 5-cm) baking tin. Stir in the remaining ingredients except the powdered sugar.

Bake for 35–40 minutes or until a wooden toothpick inserted into the center comes out clean and the top is golden brown. Remove from the oven and let cool. Sprinkle with powdered sugar.

30 MONDAY

31 TUESDAY

1 WEDNESDAY

2 THURSDAY

Imbolc,
Groundhog Day

3 FRIDAY

JANUARY 2023						
S	M	T	W	T	F	S
1	2	3	4	5	6	7
8	9	10	11	12	13	14
15	16	17	18	19	20	21
22	23	24	25	26	27	28
29	30	31				

FEBRUARY 2023						
S	M	T	W	T	F	S
			1	2	3	4
5	6	7	8	9	10	11
12	13	14	15	16	17	18
19	20	21	22	23	24	25
26	27	28				

4 SATURDAY

5 SUNDAY

Full Moon ◯

FEBRUARY 2023

Sunday	Monday	Tuesday	Wednesday
29	30	31	1
5 Full Moon ○	6	7	8
12	13 Last Quarter Moon ◐	14 Valentine's Day	15
19	20 Presidents' Day New Moon ●	21	22 Ash Wednesday
26	27 First Quarter Moon ◑	28	1

Thursday	Friday	Saturday	NOTES
2 Imbolc, Groundhog Day	3	4	
9	10	11	
16	17	18	
23	24	25	
2	3	4	

FEBRUARY 2023

6 MONDAY

7 TUESDAY

8 WEDNESDAY

9 THURSDAY

FEBRUARY 2023

S	M	T	W	T	F	S
			1	2	3	4
5	6	7	8	9	10	11
12	13	14	15	16	17	18
19	20	21	22	23	24	25
26	27	28				

10 FRIDAY

MARCH 2023

S	M	T	W	T	F	S
			1	2	3	4
5	6	7	8	9	10	11
12	13	14	15	16	17	18
19	20	21	22	23	24	25
26	27	28	29	30	31	

11 SATURDAY

12 SUNDAY

13 MONDAY

Last Quarter Moon ◑

14 TUESDAY

Valentine's Day

15 WEDNESDAY

16 THURSDAY

17 FRIDAY

FEBRUARY 2023						
S	M	T	W	T	F	S
			1	2	3	4
5	6	7	8	9	10	11
12	13	14	15	16	17	18
19	20	21	22	23	24	25
26	27	28				

18 SATURDAY

19 SUNDAY

MARCH 2023						
S	M	T	W	T	F	S
			1	2	3	4
5	6	7	8	9	10	11
12	13	14	15	16	17	18
19	20	21	22	23	24	25
26	27	28	29	30	31	

Magickal Tincture Blend for Sweet Love

Magickal workings with tinctures tap into the deep powers within our own spirits as well as the spirits of plants. The alcohol base activates the plants' spirit, allowing their energies to be infused into the tincture. Magickal tinctures need to be charged with prayers and blessings. Shake the tincture mixture two times a day to direct your energy into the jar and to activate the plants' magick. Say a prayer or blessing as you shake. This tincture is for magickal *external use* only. It can be worn as a perfume, poured into a bath, or used to anoint a candle, to sweeten love.

Ingredients

- 1 tablespoon cloves
- 1/2 cup (120 ml) aloe vera juice (liquid)
- 1/2 cup (112 g) lemon peel, dried and chopped
- 1/2 cup (112 g) orange peel, dried and chopped
- 1/2 cup (16 g) yellow dock
- 8 cups (1.9 L) alcohol

20 MONDAY

New Moon ●
Presidents' Day

21 TUESDAY

22 WEDNESDAY

Ash Wednesday

23 THURSDAY

24 FRIDAY

25 SATURDAY   **26** SUNDAY

27 MONDAY

First Quarter Moon ◐
_____

28 TUESDAY

_____

1 WEDNESDAY

_____

2 THURSDAY

FEBRUARY 2023

S	M	T	W	T	F	S
			1	2	3	4
5	6	7	8	9	10	11
12	13	14	15	16	17	18
19	20	21	22	23	24	25
26	27	28				

3 FRIDAY

MARCH 2023

S	M	T	W	T	F	S
			1	2	3	4
5	6	7	8	9	10	11
12	13	14	15	16	17	18
19	20	21	22	23	24	25
26	27	28	29	30	31	

4 SATURDAY

5 SUNDAY

MARCH 2023

Sunday	Monday	Tuesday	Wednesday
26	27	28	1
5	6	7 Full Moon ◯	8
12 Daylight Saving Time Begins (US, CAN)	13 Commonwealth Day (UK, CAN, AUS, NZ)	14 Last Quarter Moon ◑	15
19	20 Ostara (Spring Equinox)	21 New Moon ●	22 Ramadan (begins at sundown)
26	27	28 First Quarter Moon ◐	29

Thursday	Friday	Saturday
2	3	4
9	10	11
16	17	18
	St. Patrick's Day	
23	24	25
30	31	1

NOTES

6 MONDAY

---

7 TUESDAY

Full Moon ◯

---

8 WEDNESDAY

---

9 THURSDAY

---

10 FRIDAY

---

11 SATURDAY

12 SUNDAY

Daylight Saving Time
Begins (US, CAN)

MARCH 2023

13 MONDAY

Commonwealth Day (UK, CAN, AUS, NZ)

14 TUESDAY

Last Quarter Moon ◗

15 WEDNESDAY

16 THURSDAY

MARCH 2023						
S	M	T	W	T	F	S
			1	2	3	4
5	6	7	8	9	10	11
12	13	14	15	16	17	18
19	20	21	22	23	24	25
26	27	28	29	30	31	

APRIL 2023						
S	M	T	W	T	F	S
						1
2	3	4	5	6	7	8
9	10	11	12	13	14	15
16	17	18	19	20	21	22
23	24	25	26	27	28	29
30						

17 FRIDAY

St. Patrick's Day

18 SATURDAY

19 SUNDAY

OSTARA
(SPRING EQUINOX)

By Sherry, aka Phoenix Rayn Song

O stara is celebrated on the spring (vernal) equinox, [when] day and night are almost equal. . . . These celestial and terrestrial occurrences usher in the changes in nature, life, and spirit that we as Wiccans enjoy and celebrate at springtime. Spiritually speaking, spring is the season of new beginnings, fertility, and growth. The name Ostara is derived from the Germanic goddess Eostre—goddess of the dawn, spring, and fertility. . . . Eostre is associated with blooming flowers and bunny rabbits, two very traditional symbols of fecundity, as well as decorated fertility eggs. . . . On Ostara I decorate my altar with flowers, painted eggs, and rabbit statues and create a special treat as an offering to Eostre. One of my favorite things to make is a little loaf of banana bread, as it tastes and smells so incredible and adds sweetness to my offering.

Sweet Banana Bread for Ostara

Makes 1 loaf

Ingredients

- ½ cup (113 g) unsalted butter, softened
- 1 cup (200 g) sugar
- ¾ teaspoon salt
- 1 teaspoon baking soda
- ½ teaspoon vanilla
- 2 eggs
- ½ cup (120 ml) milk with 1 tablespoon vinegar added
- 2 cups (680 g) mashed banana

Cream butter and sugar in a bowl until fluffy. Stir in salt, baking soda, vanilla, and eggs, and then beat in milk-and-vinegar mixture and bananas. Bake in a greased bread pan for 60 minutes at 350°F (175°C).

MARCH 2023

20 MONDAY

21 TUESDAY

New Moon ●

22 WEDNESDAY

Ramadan (begins at sundown)

23 THURSDAY

MARCH 2023

S	M	T	W	T	F	S
			1	2	3	4
5	6	7	8	9	10	11
12	13	14	15	16	17	18
19	20	21	22	23	24	25
26	27	28	29	30	31	

24 FRIDAY

APRIL 2023

S	M	T	W	T	F	S
						1
2	3	4	5	6	7	8
9	10	11	12	13	14	15
16	17	18	19	20	21	22
23	24	25	26	27	28	29
30						

25 SATURDAY

26 SUNDAY

27 MONDAY

28 TUESDAY

First Quarter Moon

29 WEDNESDAY

30 THURSDAY

MARCH 2023						
S	M	T	W	T	F	S
			1	2	3	4
5	6	7	8	9	10	11
12	13	14	15	16	17	18
19	20	21	22	23	24	25
26	27	28	29	30	31	

31 FRIDAY

1 SATURDAY

2 SUNDAY

Palm Sunday

APRIL 2023						
S	M	T	W	T	F	S
						1
2	3	4	5	6	7	8
9	10	11	12	13	14	15
16	17	18	19	20	21	22
23	24	25	26	27	28	29
30						

APRIL 2023

Sunday	Monday	Tuesday	Wednesday
26	27	28	29
2 Palm Sunday	3	4	5 Passover (begins at sundown)
9 Easter Sunday	10 Easter Monday, Bank holiday (UK)	11	12
16 Orthodox Easter	17	18	19
23	24	25 Anzac Day (AUS, NZ)	26
30	1	2	3

Thursday	Friday	Saturday
30	31	1
6 Full Moon ◯	7 Good Friday	8
13 Last Quarter Moon ◑	14	15
20 New Moon ●	21 Eid al-Fitr (begins at sundown)	22 Earth Day
27 First Quarter Moon ◐	28	29
4	5	6

Magickal Tea Potions

Drinking magickal teas allows you to take magick inside yourself. Begin by steeping your desired herbs in hot water for 5–10 minutes, then strain. As you steep the potion, envision yourself covered in a blue or green light. As you drink the potion, visualize a blue or green light coming from the liquid. Afterward, the light will start radiating from within, throughout your whole body and out into the world—to heaven (as above) and into the earth (so below)—extending your will and desire into the universe. Here are two potions to try:

Divination

- 1/4 teaspoon goldenrod
- 1/4 teaspoon peppermint

Psychic Development

- 1/4 teaspoon calendula (marigold)
- 1/4 teaspoon ginkgo leaf
- 1/4 teaspoon lavender

APRIL 2023

3 MONDAY

4 TUESDAY

5 WEDNESDAY

Passover (begins at sundown)

6 THURSDAY

Full Moon ◯

7 FRIDAY

Good Friday

APRIL 2023

S	M	T	W	T	F	S
						1
2	3	4	5	6	7	8
9	10	11	12	13	14	15
16	17	18	19	20	21	22
23	24	25	26	27	28	29
30						

MAY 2023

S	M	T	W	T	F	S
	1	2	3	4	5	6
7	8	9	10	11	12	13
14	15	16	17	18	19	20
21	22	23	24	25	26	27
28	29	30	31			

8 SATURDAY

9 SUNDAY

Easter Sunday

10 MONDAY

Easter Monday, Bank holiday (UK)

11 TUESDAY

12 WEDNESDAY

13 THURSDAY

Last Quarter Moon ◑

14 FRIDAY

15 SATURDAY | 16 SUNDAY

Orthodox Easter

APRIL 2023

17 MONDAY

18 TUESDAY

19 WEDNESDAY

20 THURSDAY

New Moon ●

21 FRIDAY

Eid al-Fitr (begins at sundown)

22 SATURDAY

23 SUNDAY

Earth Day

Self-Love Spell

It is important to take care not only of your physical self but also of your mental well-being. This simple spell promotes self-confidence and self-love.

Materials

After-shower body lotion

Any beauty supplies you use regularly, such as skin-care products, makeup, powders, face cream, and shaving gels

Ritual

Sit on the floor or on your bed in a comfortable position and surround yourself with all of your beauty and skin-care products. Imagine that these products are covered in a pink light. Slowly start to run your hands over your body from your feet to your head. As you connect with your body, start the chant:

> *"Love within, love without,*
> *I love myself without doubt."*

After a while, you will start to feel the pink light become part of your body. At this point, begin to apply the after-shower lotion and repeat the chant. As you smooth the lotion over your skin, visualize the pink light entering you through your pores. When you have covered your body from head to toe, stand up and say loudly:

> *"I am loved."*

Continue to get ready for the day as you normally would. If at any time in the future you begin to feel less confident or a little down in the dumps, use the same after-shower lotion and repeat the procedure above. Any of the other products that were charged in the spell with pink light can also be used to instantly make you feel better about yourself.

To keep items charged, repeat the spell once a month, preferably under the new moon for growth.

APRIL 2023

24 MONDAY

25 TUESDAY

Anzac Day (AUS, NZ)

26 WEDNESDAY

27 THURSDAY

First Quarter Moon ◑

28 FRIDAY

29 SATURDAY

30 SUNDAY

APRIL 2023						
S	M	T	W	T	F	S
						1
2	3	4	5	6	7	8
9	10	11	12	13	14	15
16	17	18	19	20	21	22
23	24	25	26	27	28	29
30						

MAY 2023						
S	M	T	W	T	F	S
	1	2	3	4	5	6
7	8	9	10	11	12	13
14	15	16	17	18	19	20
21	22	23	24	25	26	27
28	29	30	31			

Sunday	Monday	Tuesday	Wednesday
30	1 Beltane, May Day (bank holiday UK, IRL)	2	3
7	8	9	10
14 Mother's Day	15	16	17
21	22 Victoria Day (CAN)	23	24
28	29 Memorial Day (US), Spring bank holiday (UK)	30	31

Thursday	Friday	Saturday
4	5	6
	Cinco de Mayo Full Moon ○	
11	12	13
	Last Quarter Moon ◑	
18	19	20
	New Moon ●	
25	26	27
		First Quarter Moon ◐
1	2	3

BELTANE

By Cheryl Croce Culver

Merry meet. When I think of the Sabbat of Beltane, I think about May baskets, trees budding out into new growth after the long winter months, and spring flowers popping forth from the frozen ground and showing us that warmth and sunshine are returning to the earth. The name *Beltane* comes from the Celtic word "Bel-fire," or "fire of the Celtic god Bel" (also called Beli, Balar, Balor, and Belenus), god of light and fire. Beltane is a time of bonfires to welcome warmth and a time for new life and fertility. It is a festival of flowers, sensuality, and delight. Everything is coming awake, and the cycle of life once again begins. Love is in the air, and it is a time to run and play and get out of our homes to seek food and fun. We have spring fever!

The most memorable and obvious symbol of Beltane is the maypole. A phallic symbol, it represents the male, stimulating force in nature, and it is used to show the sacred union between the goddess and god that takes place at this time. The pole represents the god, of course, and the earth around the pole represents the goddess.

MAY 2023

1 MONDAY

Beltane,

May Day (bank holiday UK, IRL)

2 TUESDAY

3 WEDNESDAY

4 THURSDAY

MAY 2023						
S	M	T	W	T	F	S
	1	2	3	4	5	6
7	8	9	10	11	12	13
14	15	16	17	18	19	20
21	22	23	24	25	26	27
28	29	30	31			

5 FRIDAY

Cinco de Mayo

Full Moon ◯

JUNE 2023						
S	M	T	W	T	F	S
				1	2	3
4	5	6	7	8	9	10
11	12	13	14	15	16	17
18	19	20	21	22	23	24
25	26	27	28	29	30	

6 SATURDAY

7 SUNDAY

Cheryl Croce Culver's
Cinnamon Muffins for Beltane

Beltane is associated with dairy and breads, and these muffins are one of my favorite Beltane recipes.

Makes 12 muffins

Ingredients

- ½ cup (64 g) all-purpose flour
- ½ cup (100 g) sugar
- 2 teaspoons baking powder
- ½ teaspoon sea salt
- ½ teaspoon ground nutmeg

- ¼ teaspoon ground allspice
- ½ teaspoon cinnamon
- 1 egg, beaten
- ½ cup (120 ml) milk
- ⅓ cup (76 g) butter, melted

Topping

- 2 tablespoons sugar
- ½ teaspoon ground cinnamon

- ¼ cup (57 g) butter, melted

Mix flour, sugar, baking powder, salt, nutmeg, allspice, and cinnamon. Stir egg, milk, and butter into dry ingredients until moistened. Spoon batter into greased or paper-lined muffin cups. Bake at 400°F (205°C) for 20 minutes or until a wooden toothpick inserted into the center of a muffin comes out clean.

For topping, combine the sugar and cinnamon. Brush the tops of the warm muffins with the melted butter and dip them into the sugar-and-cinnamon mixture.

MAY 2023

8 MONDAY

9 TUESDAY

10 WEDNESDAY

11 THURSDAY

12 FRIDAY

Last Quarter Moon ◑

13 SATURDAY

14 SUNDAY

Mother's Day

MAY 2023

S	M	T	W	T	F	S
	1	2	3	4	5	6
7	8	9	10	11	12	13
14	15	16	17	18	19	20
21	22	23	24	25	26	27
28	29	30	31			

JUNE 2023

S	M	T	W	T	F	S
				1	2	3
4	5	6	7	8	9	10
11	12	13	14	15	16	17
18	19	20	21	22	23	24
25	26	27	28	29	30	

15 MONDAY

---

16 TUESDAY

---

17 WEDNESDAY

---

18 THURSDAY

---

19 FRIDAY

New Moon ●

---

20 SATURDAY | **21** SUNDAY

MAY 2023

22 MONDAY

Victoria Day (CAN)

23 TUESDAY

24 WEDNESDAY

25 THURSDAY

MAY 2023						
S	M	T	W	T	F	S
	1	2	3	4	5	6
7	8	9	10	11	12	13
14	15	16	17	18	19	20
21	22	23	24	25	26	27
28	29	30	31			

26 FRIDAY

JUNE 2023						
S	M	T	W	T	F	S
				1	2	3
4	5	6	7	8	9	10
11	12	13	14	15	16	17
18	19	20	21	22	23	24
25	26	27	28	29	30	

27 SATURDAY

28 SUNDAY

First Quarter Moon ◑

29 MONDAY

Memorial Day (US), Spring bank holiday (UK)

30 TUESDAY

31 WEDNESDAY

1 THURSDAY

2 FRIDAY

MAY 2023						
S	M	T	W	T	F	S
	1	2	3	4	5	6
7	8	9	10	11	12	13
14	15	16	17	18	19	20
21	22	23	24	25	26	27
28	29	30	31			

3 SATURDAY

4 SUNDAY

Full Moon ◯

JUNE 2023						
S	M	T	W	T	F	S
				1	2	3
4	5	6	7	8	9	10
11	12	13	14	15	16	17
18	19	20	21	22	23	24
25	26	27	28	29	30	

House-Cleansing Incense Spell

This spell is for an energetic washing of your home. The herbal wash mixture helps remove negative energy and replace it with positive energy and blessings, especially appropriate for spring.

Materials

- ¼ cup (70 g) sea salt (used to absorb heat)
  Censer or a fire-safe dish
- 1 charcoal disc (the small discs used to burn incense work well)
- 2 tablespoons finely ground angelica root
- 2 tablespoons finely ground lemon balm
- 2 tablespoons finely ground elderberry flowers
  Small bowl
- 1 feather

Ritual

Sprinkle a layer of salt onto the bottom of the censer or fire-safe dish. Place the charcoal disc on the salt, and light the charcoal. While the charcoal is sparking, mix the herbs together in the bowl to create a cleansing incense.

When the edge of the entire charcoal disc is glowing light red, slowly sprinkle the cleansing incense mixture on top of it. Carefully pick up the censer or fire-safe dish and walk to the front door. As you walk, use the feather to lightly waft the smoke toward the door. "Draw" a pentacle over the front door with the smoke, using the feather. As you draw the pentacle, state:

"Be gone negativity, Here now blessed be."

JUNE 2023

Sunday	Monday	Tuesday	Wednesday
28	29	30	31
4	5	6	7
11	12	13	14 Flag Day (US)
18 Father's Day New Moon ●	19 Juneteenth	20	21 Litha (Summer Solstice)
25	26 First Quarter Moon ◐	27	28

Thursday	Friday	Saturday	NOTES
1	2	3	
8	9	10 Last Quarter Moon ◐	
15	16	17	
22	23	24	
29	30	1	

JUNE 2023

5 MONDAY

6 TUESDAY

7 WEDNESDAY

8 THURSDAY

JUNE 2022						
S	M	T	W	T	F	S
				1	2	3
4	5	6	7	8	9	10
11	12	13	14	15	16	17
18	19	20	21	22	23	24
25	26	27	28	29	30	

9 FRIDAY

JULY 2023						
S	M	T	W	T	F	S
						1
2	3	4	5	6	7	8
9	10	11	12	13	14	15
16	17	18	19	20	21	22
23	24	25	26	27	28	29
30	31					

10 SATURDAY

11 SUNDAY

Last Quarter Moon ◖

12 MONDAY

13 TUESDAY

14 WEDNESDAY

Flag Day (US)

15 THURSDAY

S	M	T	W	T	F	S
				1	2	3
4	5	6	7	8	9	10
11	12	13	14	15	16	17
18	19	20	21	22	23	24
25	26	27	28	29	30	

16 FRIDAY

17 SATURDAY

18 SUNDAY

Father's Day

New Moon

S	M	T	W	T	F	S
						1
2	3	4	5	6	7	8
9	10	11	12	13	14	15
16	17	18	19	20	21	22
23	24	25	26	27	28	29
30	31					

LITHA
(SUMMER SOLSTICE)

By Katie Snow

Litha, also known as Midsummer, is centered around the summer solstice, the longest day of the year. The exact dates vary by where you are geographically, but the holiday is typically celebrated between June 19 and June 25. The celebration of Midsummer's Eve, which predates Christianity, was the festival of the summer solstice. During these festivals, large bonfires were set to ward off the evil spirits that were believed to roam the earth freely while the sun turned toward the south. Astrologically at this time, the sun is entering Cancer, so Midsummer is not only a great time for fire magick but also water magick.

This is a good time for honoring the Oak King by having oak leaves and all the colors of summer on your altar. Litha is a time to get back to nature as the fields grow and flowers bloom. Try to spend as much time as you can outdoors, enjoying the sun that is once again warming the earth. A perfect way to celebrate is a bonfire and get-together with family and friends to share summertime fare. Litha is a joyous time of the year, full of all the fun that the summer months have to offer. Adding a drum circle or music and dancing to your celebration is a wonderful way to fully enjoy any Midsummer gathering.

19 MONDAY

Juneteenth

20 TUESDAY

21 WEDNESDAY

Litha (Summer Solstice)

22 THURSDAY

23 FRIDAY

24 SATURDAY

25 SUNDAY

JUNE/JULY 2023

26 MONDAY

First Quarter Moon ◑

27 TUESDAY

28 WEDNESDAY

29 THURSDAY

JUNE 2022						
S	M	T	W	T	F	S
				1	2	3
4	5	6	7	8	9	10
11	12	13	14	15	16	17
18	19	20	21	22	23	24
25	26	27	28	29	30	

30 FRIDAY

JULY 2023						
S	M	T	W	T	F	S
						1
2	3	4	5	6	7	8
9	10	11	12	13	14	15
16	17	18	19	20	21	22
23	24	25	26	27	28	29
30	31					

1 SATURDAY

Canada Day

2 SUNDAY

JULY 2023

Sunday	Monday	Tuesday	Wednesday
25	26	27	28
2	3 Full Moon ◯	4 Independence Day (US)	5
9 Last Quarter Moon ◐	10	11	12
16	17 New Moon ●	18	19
23	24	25 First Quarter Moon ◑	26
30	31 Lammas/Lughnasadh (begins at sundown)	1	2

Thursday	Friday	Saturday	NOTES
29	30	1 Canada Day	
6	7	8	
13	14	15	
20	21	22	
27	28	29	
3	4	5	

JULY 2023

3 MONDAY

Full Moon ○

4 TUESDAY

Independence Day (US)

5 WEDNESDAY

6 THURSDAY

JULY 2023						
S	M	T	W	T	F	S
						1
2	3	4	5	6	7	8
9	10	11	12	13	14	15
16	17	18	19	20	21	22
23	24	25	26	27	28	29
30	31					

7 FRIDAY

AUGUST 2023						
S	M	T	W	T	F	S
		1	2	3	4	5
6	7	8	9	10	11	12
13	14	15	16	17	18	19
20	21	22	23	24	25	26
27	28	29	30	31		

8 SATURDAY

9 SUNDAY

Last Quarter Moon ◐

The Power behind Plants and Crystals

When a witch works with a plant or crystal, they are working with the spirits behind those plants or crystals. The witch and spirits form spiritual alliances that can manifest in the form of animals (familiars) or other plants and crystals. Offering a prayer to the spirits of the ingredients we use is a way of honoring and acknowledging them as our allies

and asking them to help us; it also infuses potions with power for magickal work and healing, uniting the mind, body, and spirit. The prayer below can be recited before working with plants in spells. If you are working with multiple herbs, you can name them all at once or perform the prayer for each herb individually. Say the prayer with your eyes closed, with your hands palm down over the herbs for a few moments, and visualize the plant's spirit energy reacting to your spirit energy. See its spirit rise up through one hand and your spirit reach down through the other. This will seal the connection between the two of you.

Thank-You Prayer to Our Plant Allies

"To the spirit of [insert plant name here], I thank you for your sacrifice. Thank you for giving yourself to me to sustain me, heal me, help me, and protect me.
May your essence fill me with health, and may your blessings fall upon me. Spirit of [insert plant name here], may you be blessed. Thank you for your sacrifice."

JULY 2023

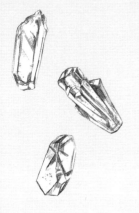

10 MONDAY

11 TUESDAY

12 WEDNESDAY

13 THURSDAY

14 FRIDAY

15 SATURDAY

16 SUNDAY

17 MONDAY

New Moon ●

18 TUESDAY

19 WEDNESDAY

20 THURSDAY

JULY 2023						
S	M	T	W	T	F	S
						1
2	3	4	5	6	7	8
9	10	11	12	13	14	15
16	17	18	19	20	21	22
23	24	25	26	27	28	29
30	31					

21 FRIDAY

AUGUST 2023						
S	M	T	W	T	F	S
		1	2	3	4	5
6	7	8	9	10	11	12
13	14	15	16	17	18	19
20	21	22	23	24	25	26
27	28	29	30	31		

22 SATURDAY

23 SUNDAY

Daily Shower Spell

This spell will set you in good stead for the day and leave you with an inner peace, a sense of clarity, and the stamina to embrace the moment.

Materials

Water

Shampoo and conditioner

Soap or shower gel

Ritual

Start the shower with the water as hot as you can stand it, and step inside. Once inside the shower, let the water run over you from head to toe. As you bathe, watch the water going down the drain and picture it in your mind as a gray color. Next, visualize the water removing all of your anxieties and any issues you had from the day before.

Begin to wash your hair with shampoo. In your mind's eye, see the stress and anxiety leaving your body and entering into the shampoo bubbles. Repeat the visualization process with the conditioner. Take the soap or shower gel and, starting with your face, wash your whole body several times, cleansing from head to toe. As you lather, say these words over and over:

"Water, water, wash away. Water, water, cleanse today."

Once you are clean, rinse off all of the suds. The lather will absorb your troubles and wash them down the drain. Cool the shower temperature slightly, and bathe for a few more minutes in the refreshing water. When you feel comfortably cleansed and refreshed, step out and dry off with a towel from top to bottom while repeating these words:

"By the earth in the soap,
By the air in the steam,
By the fire which heats the water,
By the water that washes,
I am cleansed, clean, and ready for the day."

24 MONDAY

---

25 TUESDAY

First Quarter Moon ◗

26 WEDNESDAY

---

27 THURSDAY

---

28 FRIDAY

---

29 SATURDAY | **30** SUNDAY

AUGUST 2023

Sunday	Monday	Tuesday	Wednesday
30	31	1 Full Moon ○	2
6	7	8 Last Quarter Moon ◑	9
13	14	15	16 New Moon ●
20	21	22	23
27	28 Summer bank holiday (UK)	29	30

Thursday	Friday	Saturday
3	4	5
10	11	12
17	18	19
24	25	26
31	1	2

First Quarter Moon ◐

JULY/AUGUST 2023

31 MONDAY

Lammas/Lughnasadh (begins at sundown)

1 TUESDAY

Full Moon ◯

2 WEDNESDAY

3 THURSDAY

JULY 2023						
S	M	T	W	T	F	S
						1
2	3	4	5	6	7	8
9	10	11	12	13	14	15
16	17	18	19	20	21	22
23	24	25	26	27	28	29
30	31					

4 FRIDAY

AUGUST 2023						
S	M	T	W	T	F	S
		1	2	3	4	5
6	7	8	9	10	11	12
13	14	15	16	17	18	19
20	21	22	23	24	25	26
27	28	29	30	31		

5 SATURDAY

6 SUNDAY

Magickal Loaf of Bread

There's nothing more comforting than the smell of bread baking in the oven, and this magickal loaf will make everyone in the family happy.

Makes 1 loaf

Ingredients

- 1 sprig fresh rosemary, stem removed
- 1 sprig fresh oregano
- 1 sprig fresh thyme
- 4 cups (544 g) bread flour
- 1 teaspoon salt
- 1 packet instant yeast

- 2 tablespoons superfine baker's sugar
- 3 tablespoons olive oil
- 1⅓ cups (360 ml) water, or enough to bring the dough together
- 7 white candles

Chop the herbs and mix them together in a bowl. Place each of the other ingredients in separate bowls. Light a white candle next to them. Say the following spell once:

"Bless this food, these magickal gifts,
Our mood is bright with every bite."

Mix all the dry ingredients in a bowl, then make a well in the center and pour in the oil and water. Stir together and then tip out onto a floured surface and knead for 15 minutes, stretching and pulling. While kneading, repeat the spell above, over and over.

Grease a bowl and place the dough inside it. Cover with plastic wrap or a clean towel. Let the dough rise in a warm place for 1 hour and then punch it back and knead it for another 15 minutes. While kneading, repeat the spell.

Move the bread to a greased tin and leave it to rise for another hour; meanwhile, preheat your oven to 350°F (175°C). Place the dough in the oven, and bake for 20–30 minutes.

AUGUST 2023

7 MONDAY

---

8 TUESDAY

Last Quarter Moon ◑

---

9 WEDNESDAY

---

10 THURSDAY

11 FRIDAY

---

12 SATURDAY

13 SUNDAY

AUGUST 2023

14 MONDAY

15 TUESDAY

16 WEDNESDAY

New Moon ●

17 THURSDAY

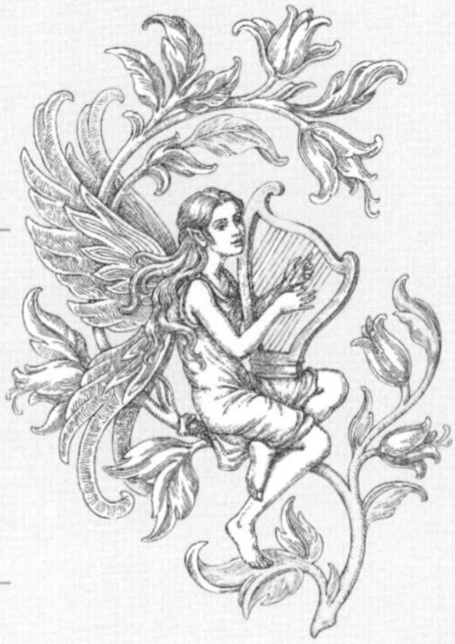

18 FRIDAY

19 SATURDAY

20 SUNDAY

21 MONDAY

22 TUESDAY

23 WEDNESDAY

24 THURSDAY

First Quarter Moon ◑

25 FRIDAY

26 SATURDAY

27 SUNDAY

AUGUST 2023

S	M	T	W	T	F	S
		1	2	3	4	5
6	7	8	9	10	11	12
13	14	15	16	17	18	19
20	21	22	23	24	25	26
27	28	29	30	31		

SEPTEMBER 2023

S	M	T	W	T	F	S
					1	2
3	4	5	6	7	8	9
10	11	12	13	14	15	16
17	18	19	20	21	22	23
24	25	26	27	28	29	30

AUGUST/SEPTEMBER 2023

28 MONDAY

Summer bank holiday (UK)

29 TUESDAY

30 WEDNESDAY

Full Moon ○

31 THURSDAY

AUGUST 2023						
S	M	T	W	T	F	S
		1	2	3	4	5
6	7	8	9	10	11	12
13	14	15	16	17	18	19
20	21	22	23	24	25	26
27	28	29	30	31		

1 FRIDAY

SEPTEMBER 2023						
S	M	T	W	T	F	S
					1	2
3	4	5	6	7	8	9
10	11	12	13	14	15	16
17	18	19	20	21	22	23
24	25	26	27	28	29	30

2 SATURDAY

3 SUNDAY

SEPTEMBER 2023

Sunday	Monday	Tuesday	Wednesday
27	28	29	30
3	4 Labor Day (US, CAN)	5	6 Last Quarter Moon
10	11	12	13
17	18	19	20
24 Yom Kippur (begins at sundown)	25	26	27

Thursday	Friday	Saturday
31	1	2
7	8	9
14 New Moon ●	15 Rosh Hashanah (begins at sundown)	16
21	22 Mabon (Autumnal Equinox) First Quarter Moon ◐	23
28	29 Full Moon ○	30

4 MONDAY

Labor Day (US, CAN)

5 TUESDAY

6 WEDNESDAY

Last Quarter Moon ◑

7 THURSDAY

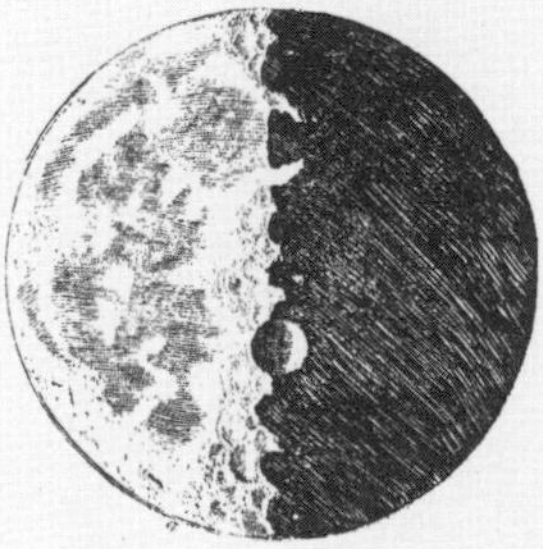

8 FRIDAY

9 SATURDAY

10 SUNDAY

SEPTEMBER 2023

11 MONDAY

12 TUESDAY

13 WEDNESDAY

14 THURSDAY

New Moon ●

15 FRIDAY

Rosh Hashanah (begins at sundown)

16 SATURDAY

17 SUNDAY

MABON
(AUTUMNAL EQUINOX)
By Lori Hayes, aka Darklady

Mabon, to me, means the first day of fall, when the days and nights are the same length and winter will soon be here. It's celebrated at the autumnal equinox, the midpoint between harvesting and sowing crops, when we should give thanks as well as look back on the past year and plan for the coming one. Mabon is also a time of rest and celebration, a time for spells of protection, prosperity, security, and self-confidence. The colors to use are gold, orange, yellow, red, bronze, and rust. I set up an altar indoors using a small, round table. On my altar are acorns and leaves that I've collected, along with corn. . . . I light a yellow-and-orange candle and ask for blessings to come into my life and for peace in the world. Then it's time to fix my Mabon meal, sausage soup—it's wicked good. After we all sit down and give thanks to the goddess and eat, I always go for a walk in the woods or by the river—not only to walk off the dinner, but also so I can breathe and be closer to nature. Blessings to all of you.

Darklady's Mabon Sausage Soup

Serves 6 to 8

Ingredients

- 3 sausages (I like it with a kick, so I use hot sausage)
- 3 medium white onions
- 3 large cans kidney beans

- 3 large cans stewed, chopped tomatoes
- 8 small Yukon Gold potatoes
- Bay leaf, thyme, garlic powder
- Salt and pepper to taste

Heat the sausage and onions in a large soup pot until very well cooked. Add the other ingredients, and simmer until potatoes are tender. Serve in a bowl with your favorite French or sourdough bread.

SEPTEMBER 2023

18 MONDAY

---

19 TUESDAY

---

20 WEDNESDAY

21 THURSDAY

---

22 FRIDAY

Mabon (Autumnal Equinox)

First Quarter Moon ◗

23 SATURDAY

24 SUNDAY

Yom Kippur
(begins at sundown)

25 MONDAY

---

26 TUESDAY

---

27 WEDNESDAY

---

28 THURSDAY

---

29 FRIDAY

Full Moon ○

---

30 SATURDAY | **1** SUNDAY

SEPTEMBER 2023						
S	M	T	W	T	F	S
					1	2
3	4	5	6	7	8	9
10	11	12	13	14	15	16
17	18	19	20	21	22	23
24	25	26	27	28	29	30

OCTOBER 2023						
S	M	T	W	T	F	S
1	2	3	4	5	6	7
8	9	10	11	12	13	14
15	16	17	18	19	20	21
22	23	24	25	26	27	28
29	30	31				

OCTOBER 2023

Sunday	Monday	Tuesday	Wednesday
1	2	3	4
8	9 Indigenous Peoples' Day, Columbus Day (US), Thanksgiving (CAN)	10	11
15	16	17	18
22	23	24	25
29	30	31 Samhain, Halloween	1

Thursday	Friday	Saturday
5	6	7
	Last Quarter Moon ◐	
12	13	14
		New Moon ●
19	20	21
		First Quarter Moon ◑
26	27	28
		Full Moon ○
2	3	4

OCTOBER 2023

2 MONDAY

3 TUESDAY

4 WEDNESDAY

5 THURSDAY

6 FRIDAY

Last Quarter Moon ◑

7 SATURDAY

8 SUNDAY

9 MONDAY

Indigenous Peoples' Day,
Columbus Day (US),
Thanksgiving (CAN)

---

10 TUESDAY

---

11 WEDNESDAY

---

12 THURSDAY

OCTOBER 2023						
S	M	T	W	T	F	S
1	2	3	4	5	6	7
8	9	10	11	12	13	14
15	16	17	18	19	20	21
22	23	24	25	26	27	28
29	30	31				

13 FRIDAY

---

14 SATURDAY

15 SUNDAY

New Moon ●

NOVEMBER 2023						
S	M	T	W	T	F	S
			1	2	3	4
5	6	7	8	9	10	11
12	13	14	15	16	17	18
19	20	21	22	23	24	25
26	27	28	29	30		

Four Thieves Vinegar

Four Thieves Vinegar has a few different health benefits, from boosting the immune system to speeding up recovery from a cold or flu. This vinegar is a truly holistic remedy: it treats spiritual issues (cleansing and removing spiritual toxins) as well as physical issues (the garlic, herbs, and spices have multiple healing and detoxifying properties). In *Rosemary Gladstar's Medicinal Herbs,* American herbalist Rosemary Gladstar notes that this vinegar was historically used by gypsies and witches to protect against spells and witchcraft, as well as to protect their homes against thieves. Other traditions, such as hoodoo and ceremonial magick, have employed this tonic for removing and banishing negative forces and for spiritual cleansing.

Ingredients

- 5 cloves garlic, chopped or minced
- ½ cup rosemary, fresh and chopped
- 4 tablespoons lavender, dried
- 2 tablespoons hyssop
- 1 tablespoon cayenne pepper
- 1 tablespoon black peppercorn
- 4 cups (960 ml) apple cider vinegar

Place the garlic, herbs, and spices in a glass jar 1 quart (960 ml) in size or larger. Slightly warm the apple cider vinegar and pour over the mixture in the jar. Stir or shake well and let sit for four to six weeks in a cool, dark place. When ready, strain the vinegar through cheesecloth into a new bottle.

DOSAGE: For prevention, take 1 tablespoon daily as needed during cold and flu season. When sick, take 1 tablespoon two to three times daily to help speed up recovery.

16 MONDAY

17 TUESDAY

18 WEDNESDAY

19 THURSDAY

20 FRIDAY

21 SATURDAY

22 SUNDAY

First Quarter Moon ◑

OCTOBER 2023

23 MONDAY

24 TUESDAY

25 WEDNESDAY

26 THURSDAY

OCTOBER 2023						
S	M	T	W	T	F	S
1	2	3	4	5	6	7
8	9	10	11	12	13	14
15	16	17	18	19	20	21
22	23	24	25	26	27	28
29	30	31				

27 FRIDAY

NOVEMBER 2023						
S	M	T	W	T	F	S
			1	2	3	4
5	6	7	8	9	10	11
12	13	14	15	16	17	18
19	20	21	22	23	24	25
26	27	28	29	30		

28 SATURDAY

29 SUNDAY

Full Moon ◯

OCTOBER/NOVEMBER 2023

30 MONDAY

31 TUESDAY

Samhain,
Halloween

1 WEDNESDAY

2 THURSDAY

OCTOBER 2023						
S	M	T	W	T	F	S
1	2	3	4	5	6	7
8	9	10	11	12	13	14
15	16	17	18	19	20	21
22	23	24	25	26	27	28
29	30	31				

3 FRIDAY

NOVEMBER 2023						
S	M	T	W	T	F	S
			1	2	3	4
5	6	7	8	9	10	11
12	13	14	15	16	17	18
19	20	21	22	23	24	25
26	27	28	29	30		

4 SATURDAY

5 SUNDAY

Daylight Saving Time Ends
(US, CAN)

Last Quarter Moon ◗

NOVEMBER 2023

Sunday	Monday	Tuesday	Wednesday
29	30	31	1
5 Daylight Saving Time Ends (US, CAN) Last Quarter Moon ◗	6	7 Election Day (US)	8
12	13 New Moon ●	14	15
19	20 First Quarter Moon ◗	21	22
26	27 Full Moon ○	28	29

Thursday	Friday	Saturday	NOTES
2	3	4	
9	10	11 Veterans Day (US)	
16	17	18	
23	24	25	
30	1	2	

NOVEMBER 2023

6 MONDAY

7 TUESDAY

Election Day (US)

8 WEDNESDAY

9 THURSDAY

NOVEMBER 2023

S	M	T	W	T	F	S
			1	2	3	4
5	6	7	8	9	10	11
12	13	14	15	16	17	18
19	20	21	22	23	24	25
26	27	28	29	30		

10 FRIDAY

DECEMBER 2023

S	M	T	W	T	F	S
					1	2
3	4	5	6	7	8	9
10	11	12	13	14	15	16
17	18	19	20	21	22	23
24	25	26	27	28	29	30
31						

11 SATURDAY

12 SUNDAY

Veterans Day (US)

13 MONDAY

New Moon ●

14 TUESDAY

15 WEDNESDAY

16 THURSDAY

17 FRIDAY

NOVEMBER 2023						
S	M	T	W	T	F	S
			1	2	3	4
5	6	7	8	9	10	11
12	13	14	15	16	17	18
19	20	21	22	23	24	25
26	27	28	29	30		

DECEMBER 2023						
S	M	T	W	T	F	S
					1	2
3	4	5	6	7	8	9
10	11	12	13	14	15	16
17	18	19	20	21	22	23
24	25	26	27	28	29	30
31						

18 SATURDAY

19 SUNDAY

Sabbat Wish Powder to Attract Good Fortune

By Rachel McGirr

Witches across the world believe that the Sabbats hold a great power and cast spells to replenish the good things in life for the months ahead. Many witches make wish powder during Sabbats so that they have something on hand should they need it in a hurry. Wish powder works for any desire, as long as it's not grounded in greed. It's very general, but handy when you want to cast some magick quickly.

Materials

- 1 tall, white, tapered candle with candleholder
- 3 teaspoons dried meadowsweet (lucky Lammas herb, can be purchased online)
- 3 teaspoons of dried mint
- 3 teaspoons dried basil
- Mortar and pestle
- 1 small pot of silver glitter to enhance magick and represent wishes
- 1 small plastic container with a snap-on lid

Ritual

On one of the evenings during the Sabbat you're celebrating, light the candle and place it in the candleholder. Grind the herbs as finely as you can, using a pestle and mortar. Then, add the small pot of glitter, and mix in well. Transfer the mixture to the plastic container and seal the lid. Hold the container in one hand and the candle in the other, and say these words seven times:

> *"Magickal powder in this dish,*
> *Be ever powerful, grant my wish."*

Leave the powder next to the candle for several hours (making sure not to leave the candle unattended), and then snuff the candle out. Store the powder under your altar or with your other magickal tools. Whenever you want to make a wish, bring the wish powder outside at night. Take a pinch and throw it into the night while silently making your wish. Be realistic with your wishes, and they should come to fruition.

20 MONDAY

First Quarter Moon ◑

---

21 TUESDAY

---

22 WEDNESDAY

---

23 THURSDAY

Thanksgiving (US)

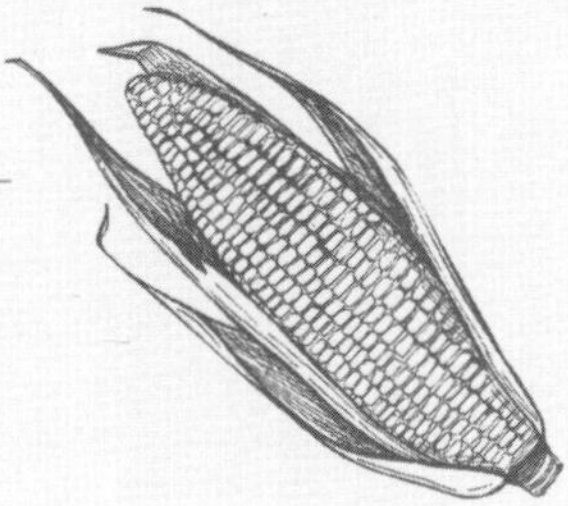

---

24 FRIDAY

---

25 SATURDAY | **26** SUNDAY

27 MONDAY

Full Moon ○

28 TUESDAY

29 WEDNESDAY

30 THURSDAY

NOVEMBER 2023						
S	M	T	W	T	F	S
			1	2	3	4
5	6	7	8	9	10	11
12	13	14	15	16	17	18
19	20	21	22	23	24	25
26	27	28	29	30		

1 FRIDAY

DECEMBER 2023						
S	M	T	W	T	F	S
					1	2
3	4	5	6	7	8	9
10	11	12	13	14	15	16
17	18	19	20	21	22	23
24	25	26	27	28	29	30
31						

2 SATURDAY

3 SUNDAY

Sunday	Monday	Tuesday	Wednesday
26	27	28	29
3	4	5 Last Quarter Moon ◑	6
10	11	12 New Moon ●	13
17	18	19 First Quarter Moon ◑	20
24	25 Christmas Day	26 Kwanzaa, Boxing Day (CAN) Full Moon ○	27
31	1	2	3

Thursday	Friday	Saturday
30	1	2
7 Hanukkah (begins at sundown)	8	9
14	15	16
21 Yule (Winter Solstice)	22	23
28	29	30
4	5	6

4 MONDAY

5 TUESDAY

Last Quarter Moon ◑

6 WEDNESDAY

7 THURSDAY

Hanukkah (begins at sundown)

8 FRIDAY

DECEMBER 2023

S	M	T	W	T	F	S
					1	2
3	4	5	6	7	8	9
10	11	12	13	14	15	16
17	18	19	20	21	22	23
24	25	26	27	28	29	30
31						

JANUARY 2024

S	M	T	W	T	F	S
	1	2	3	4	5	6
7	8	9	10	11	12	13
14	15	16	17	18	19	20
21	22	23	24	25	26	27
28	29	30	31			

9 SATURDAY

10 SUNDAY

11 MONDAY

12 TUESDAY

New Moon ●

13 WEDNESDAY

14 THURSDAY

15 FRIDAY

DECEMBER 2023						
S	M	T	W	T	F	S
					1	2
3	4	5	6	7	8	9
10	11	12	13	14	15	16
17	18	19	20	21	22	23
24	25	26	27	28	29	30
31						

16 SATURDAY

17 SUNDAY

JANUARY 2024						
S	M	T	W	T	F	S
	1	2	3	4	5	6
7	8	9	10	11	12	13
14	15	16	17	18	19	20
21	22	23	24	25	26	27
28	29	30	31			

Magickal Spirituality

Spellcraft is just one of the magickal tools in a witch's tool kit. Those who practice magickal spirituality are just like anyone else who follows a faith. Prayers are wishes and petitions for changes or needs that are spoken without any other direct ritual actions. Spells are petitions or prayers with actions taken to obtain your desire—such as writing your name on a candle, tying knots, and so on. (You can end either a prayer or a spell with "So mote it be" if you wish.)

Many spellcasters like to invoke the power of angels. There are trillions of angels in the spirit world, each one with the power to help any problematic situation that may arise. One of the most powerful is the archangel Raphael. He is the predominant healer in the angelic realm, and many people find that when they call upon his power, their spells are more successful and their prayers are answered. To invoke his power, you could place a white feather on your workspace and say this incantation before you begin casting your spell:

> *"Archangel Raphael, healer of mankind,*
> *I ask your assistance this day.*
> *Encircle me with your powerful light,*
> *Love and protect me, come what may.*
> *Envelop me with the warmth of your wings,*
> *As I cast this spell while the angel sings."*

DECEMBER 2023

18 MONDAY

19 TUESDAY

First Quarter Moon

20 WEDNESDAY

21 THURSDAY

Yule (Winter Solstice)

22 FRIDAY

DECEMBER 2023

S	M	T	W	T	F	S
					1	2
3	4	5	6	7	8	9
10	11	12	13	14	15	16
17	18	19	20	21	22	23
24	25	26	27	28	29	30
31						

JANUARY 2024

S	M	T	W	T	F	S
	1	2	3	4	5	6
7	8	9	10	11	12	13
14	15	16	17	18	19	20
21	22	23	24	25	26	27
28	29	30	31			

23 SATURDAY

24 SUNDAY

Charity Bedell's Tourtière (Meat Pie)

This family recipe is for a pork-based pie that is perfect for Yule and Christmas. Pork was often eaten and sacrificed at Yule to the Norse god Freyr. My family typically serves this on Christmas Day for breakfast.

Serves 6 to 8

Ingredients

½ tablespoon butter or olive oil
1 pound (450 g) ground pork
2 medium-to-large onions, diced
Salt, pepper, and cinnamon
   to taste

2 potatoes of any type, boiled or
   microwaved to softness, then
   mashed
Pie crust top and bottom
   (store-bought is fine)
Mustard to taste, if desired

Grease a large, deep pan with butter or olive oil. Sauté the meat, onions, and spices together in the pan and simmer covered for 2 hours on medium-to-low heat, stirring frequently.

Preheat the oven to 375°F (190°C). Add cooked potatoes to the meat mixture and loosely fold in. Place the bottom pie crust in an ungreased glass pie pan. Fill with the meat-and-potato mixture. Cover with the top crust, using a fork to seal the two crusts together.

Place the pie in the oven and bake for 25 minutes or until golden brown. Serve warm, with mustard on top, if desired.

DECEMBER 2023

25 MONDAY

Christmas Day

26 TUESDAY

Kwanzaa, Boxing Day (CAN)

Full Moon ◯

27 WEDNESDAY

28 THURSDAY

DECEMBER 2023						
S	M	T	W	T	F	S
					1	2
3	4	5	6	7	8	9
10	11	12	13	14	15	16
17	18	19	20	21	22	23
24	25	26	27	28	29	30
31						

29 FRIDAY

JANUARY 2024						
S	M	T	W	T	F	S
	1	2	3	4	5	6
7	8	9	10	11	12	13
14	15	16	17	18	19	20
21	22	23	24	25	26	27
28	29	30	31			

30 SATURDAY

31 SUNDAY

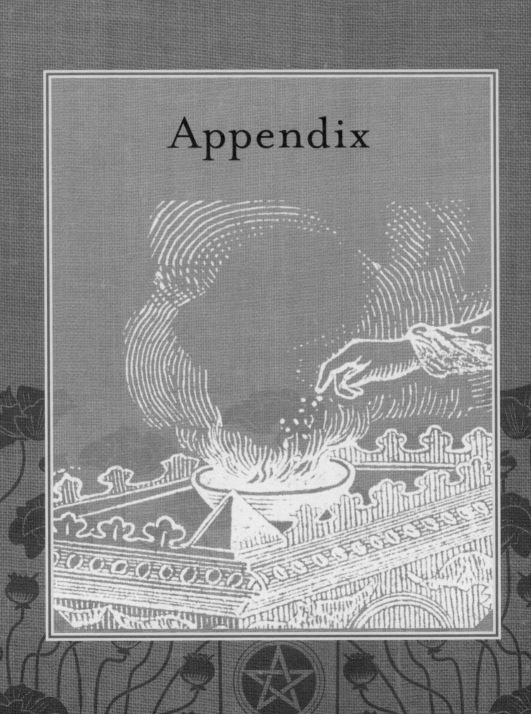

Appendix

MAGICKAL ESSENTIAL OILS

Aromatherapy can heal not only the body and mind but also the spirit, and it can be a potent ally in magickal practice as well. The scent of the herbs and oils together triggers changes deep within us, on the spiritual level. This is tremendously powerful and can be a catalyst for change.

In magick, just as in healing, herbs and oils have multiple properties and associations. Some herbs are stronger magickally than others. Magick is very personal, and what works for one person may not work for another. By developing your skills and knowledge about herbs and other plants, you will discover the ones that resonate best and are most compatible with you.

Magickal oils may not have the most pleasant scents, which is fine! The magick in the oils derives from the energetic properties of the herbs. When you are blending oils, incenses, and baths for magickal and spiritual work, let your intuition guide you. If a particular herb seems to make more sense in a blend than the one you "think" should be included, use it. Your personal guidance and the plant's spirit are talking to you. **Listen!**

Essential oils can be used individually in spells or rituals. In casting a love spell, you could anoint yourself with rose or patchouli oil to attract love and bring sensual energy to a situation. If you are having a hard time meditating, you could apply a few drops of frankincense or myrrh oil to your forehead and temples. If you are trying to attract money, a bit of basil oil on a green candle could do the trick. The following list provides several common essential oils and the attributes and areas that they correspond to when used in spells:

ALLSPICE: Money and wealth, luck, business success, health

BASIL: Happiness, peace, money, aid in meditation and trance work

BAY LEAF: Psychic awareness, purification

BLACK PEPPER: Mental alertness, protection, physical energy, courage, exorcism

CATNIP: Happiness, peace, beauty,

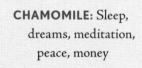

CHAMOMILE: Sleep, dreams, meditation, peace, money

CINNAMON: Physical energy, psychic awareness, prosperity

CLOVE: Healing, memory, protection, courage

EUCALYPTUS: Health, purification

FRANKINCENSE: Spirituality, meditation

GERANIUM: Happiness, protection

GINGER: Magickal energy, igniting sexual passion, love, money, courage

JUNIPER BERRIES: Purification, protection, healing

LAVENDER: Health, love, celibacy, conscious mind

LEMON: Health, purification

LEMON BALM: Peace, money, purification

LEMONGRASS: Purification, psychic awareness

LIME: Purification, protection

MARIGOLD: Health, psychic dreams, comfort, financial security and success

MUGWORT: Psychic awareness, psychic dreams, astral projection, spirituality

MYRRH: Spirituality, meditation, healing

NUTMEG: Magickal energy, psychic awareness, money

PATCHOULI: Igniting sexual passion, love, fertility, money, jinx-breaking

PEPPERMINT: Purification, aid in meditation and trance work, focus

PINE: Healing, protection, purification, money

ROSE: Igniting sexual passion, love, romance, peace, beauty

ROSEMARY: Longevity, memory, love, aid in meditation and trance work

SANDALWOOD: Spirituality, meditation, igniting sexual passion, healing

SPEARMINT: Healing, protection during sleep, strength of mind

TEA TREE: Strength; cleansing; wards off unwanted spiritual attention, negativity, hexes, and curses; healing, protection

THYME: Courage, aid in meditation and trance work, health

YLANG-YLANG: Peace, igniting sexual passion, love

CRYSTAL MAGICK

When it comes to crystals, we are attracted to them partly for their colors and the way we react to those colors. In spiritual work, colors have a very rich history of use—blue is common for healing, and red is universal for love and passion. The colors that a crystal emanates give you insight into how you can work with it magickally. Here is a simple list of color associations:

WHITE: Pure spirit, innocence, blank slate (any purpose)

RED: Love, life, sex, romance, power element of fire

ORANGE: Success, memory, gaining energy

GREEN: Money, fertility, success, growth, life-earth element

BLUE: Healing, peace, dream work

GOLD: Money, success, Sun God

YELLOW: Success, luck, element of air

SILVER: Intuition, money, psychic ability, Moon Goddess

PURPLE: Intuition, psychic energy, mental focus, spirituality

BLACK: Protection, grounding, strength

Now let us look at some crystals and their magickal associations:

AMETHYST: Dreams, healing, psychic ability, peace, love, protection against thieves, courage, happiness

AVENTURINE: Mental focus and psychic ability, eyesight, gambling and general luck, money, peace, healing

BLOODSTONE: Healing, victory, courage, success in legal matters and business, wealth

CARNELIAN: Peace, relief from depression

CITRINE: Success, protection, anti-nightmare, psychic ability

CLEAR QUARTZ: Boosts any other crystals or herbs, spirituality, protection, healing, psychic ability, power

DIAMOND: Spirituality, reconciliation, help with sexual dysfunction, protection, courage, peace, love, healing, strength

EMERALD: Love, money, mental focus and psychic ability, protection, exorcism, eyesight

FLUORITE: Mental focus and psychic ability

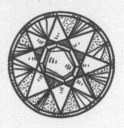

GARNET: Healing, protection, strength

HEMATITE: Grounding, healing, divination

IRON PYRITE (FOOL'S GOLD): Money, divination, luck

JADEITE: Love, healing, longevity, wisdom, protection, prosperity, money

JET: Protection, anti-nightmare, luck, divination, health

LABRADORITE: Peace of mind, peace, happiness, tranquility, relaxation

LAPIS LAZULI: Healing, joy, love, fidelity, psychic ability, protection, courage

MALACHITE: Power, protection, love, peace, business success

MOONSTONE: Love, divination, psychic ability, gardening, youth, protection, dieting, Moon Goddess

MOSS AGATE: Gardening, riches, happiness, long life, fertility

RED JASPER: Protection against poison and negativity, curing fevers, healing, beauty, grace

ROSE QUARTZ: Love, open-heart chakra, peace, happiness

RUBY: Wealth, protection, power, joy, anti-nightmare

SMOKY QUARTZ: Grounding, relief from depression

SUNSTONE: Protection, energy, health, sexual energy, Sun God

TIGER'S-EYE: Money, prosperity, courage, energy, luck, divination

Simple Crystal Magick

One of the best ways to work with crystals in magick is to simply carry them in your pocket or place them somewhere hidden but where the energy can still be effective. Ancient warriors carried bloodstones as charms for victory and to help with bleeding injuries during battle. By carrying tiger's-eye in your pocket, you can bring an increase in luck and prosperity. If you are starting to feel fatigued, touch the stone and you'll get energized. If you are running a small business, place a small malachite stone and an iron pyrite stone behind the register to attract customers and boost sales. If you place moss agate in your garden, it will be much healthier and more fertile.

"May the crystal light guide you into health and wellness."

Boosting Your Crystal Power: A Simple Cleansing Ritual

Before you begin to work with crystals, you need to cleanse them. This cleansing is both physical and energetic. It will remove any dust or dirt that may have accumulated over time in storage. The more important reason for the cleansing, however, is to remove the energy of anyone else who has handled them, allowing only your energy and the crystal's energy to remain.

Materials

Your crystals

Bowl of soapy water

Sea salt (in a small bowl)

Bowl of cold water

Ritual

Take all of your crystals and place them in the bowl of soapy water. As you wash them, visualize all the energy of others removed and only your energy remaining. As you wash them chant:

> *"Water cleanse and clean*
> *Remove the negative unseen."*

When they feel lighter, individually place them in the bowl of salt. The salt will ground them in your energy and their energy and remove any remaining extraneous energy.

Next dip them in the bowl of cold water to rinse off the salt but keep the energy infused in the crystals. As you remove them from the water, state:

> *"By the water no more negativity*
> *By the water blessed be."*

Your crystals are now blessed and cleansed. They are ready to be used.

CANDLE COLORS AND THEIR MAGICKAL CORRESPONDENCES

One of the most important parts of candle magick is using the right color candle, as the correct color will often make all the difference to the outcome. Some spells are rigid and need a precise color or shade of a color, while others are more open-ended. If you are in doubt about what color to use, always use a white candle. This is a neutral and pure color candle that can be used when you are not sure of what color would be best for a spell or if you are out of the color candle specified in your spell. Here is a list of the main candle colors and their correspondences:

WHITE
Cleansing homes
Purifying spaces
Creating harmony
Invoking spirits
Improving communication with others
Summoning guides and angels
For use in every situation

BLUE
Promoting restful sleep
Finding out the truth
Gaining wisdom
  and knowledge
Invoking psychic
  visions
Calming down
  emotions
Suppressing anger
Meditation aid

Moving into a new house
Becoming more patient with others
Curing a fever
Gaining insight
Protection

RED
Promoting strength and vigor
Rejuvenating energy and stamina
Conjuring willpower
Summoning courage
Inciting passion and sexual love
Sparking enthusiasm
Prompting quick results
Warding off enemies
Becoming more attractive to others

PINK
Healing emotions
Attracting romance

Becoming more
caring

Inviting peace and
tranquility

Healing rifts

Banishing selfish
emotions

Protecting family and friendships

Invoking spiritual healing

Being more compassionate

GREEN

Accumulating
money and
wealth

Promoting
prosperity and
abundance

Accomplishing goals

Growing plants

Attracting luck

Negotiating employment matters
and finding new jobs

Hastening conception and solving
fertility issues

Casting out greed and
resentment

YELLOW

Increasing activity

Resolving health matters

Nurturing creativity and
imagination

Passing exams and learning

Aiding concentration

Controlling mood
swings

Protecting yourself when
traveling

Persuading others

ORANGE

Increasing energy and
stamina

Improving the mind and
memory

Promoting success and luck

Developing business and career

Helping those with new jobs

Clarifying legal matters and justice

Selling goods or houses

Capturing a thief or recovering
lost property

Removing fear

PURPLE

Summoning spirit help

Bringing peace, tranquility,
and harmony

Improving psychic ability

Aiding astral projection

Healing

Easing sadness

Improving male energy

Summoning spiritual
protection

BROWN

Attuning with the
trees and
the earth

Promoting
concentration

Helping with decisiveness

Protecting animals

Amplifying assertiveness

Aiding friendships

Bringing material gain

Gaining mental stability

Connecting with Mother Nature

Studying and learning

SILVER

Summoning the Mother Goddess

Drawing down the moon

Connecting with lunar
animals

Purifying female energy

Improving all psychic
abilities

Aiding clairvoyance and
the unconscious mind

Ridding yourself of negativity

Developing intuition

Interpreting messages in dreams

Banishing bad habits

GOLD

Healing and
enhancing well-
being

Rejuvenating yourself

Improving intelligence

Bringing financial gain
and wealth

Winning competitions

Attracting love and
happiness

Maintaining peace in families

Cosmic ordering

BLACK

Protection

Strength

Banishing

Reversal

Hex-breaking

Choosing and Cleansing Your Candles

It is important for you to magickally disinfect your candles before use. It's best to make your own candles from scratch, but few of us have the time or the equipment to do this. Store-bought candles are perfectly acceptable, but try to avoid ones that are dipped, meaning that the maker dipped a white candle in colored wax. For magickal purposes, it's far better to use the ones that are a solid color throughout. There are many different ways to cleanse your candles before a spell. Some people enjoy a prolonged ceremony of candle cleansing and will go to great lengths, even leaving the candle outside for a week in the garden to soak up the moon's rays. Others just want to do a minimum amount of preparation. Below is an example of candle cleansing, also called "anointing," that sits somewhere in the middle and works perfectly well.

Step 1: Wipe clean

Wipe the wax clean with a paper towel.

Step 2: Prepare a solution

Purchase a small bottle of spring water and pour into a saucepan. Add 1 teaspoon of sea salt and warm until the salt dissolves. Allow the water to cool before pouring it back into the bottle. You can keep this water in the fridge for about a month for reuse in the future.

Step 3: Intent

Standing in front of the sink, hold the candle in your left hand, which is nearer to your heart. Being careful not to wet the wick, pour a small amount of the water over the candle. If you are using a tealight candle, remove the candle from its casing before cleansing with the water. Take a fresh paper towel and dry thoroughly while saying the following invocation:

"This magickal water cleanses thee,
With good intent and purity."

Step 4: Inscribe

With a small, sharp paring knife or a thick needle, scratch your full name and your wish into the wax. It can be anywhere on the candle, and does not need to be legible. Once the candle is lit, these words will burn away, giving the spell more clout.

Step 5: Anoint

Pour some pure vegetable (cooking) oil into a small bowl; for spells relating to health and well-being, you can mix in a few drops of other oils if you wish. Lavender is often used with healing and well-being spells to intensify the magick. Hold the candle in your left hand again. Dip the first finger of your right hand into the oil and run it down the candle from top to bottom in a line. To anoint a tealight, place it back in its casing, dip your finger into the oil, and smear it in a clockwork motion around the top of the candle wax. Say this invocation:

"This magickal oil anoints thee,
With all things good, magickally."*

The candle is now cleansed, charged, and ready to be placed in a suitable holder in preparation for your spell.

Step 6: End the spell

Choose one of the phrases below to say before looking upward and saying thank you.

"And so it is." / "The spell is cast." / "So mote it be."

*Note: One of the ways we can add more punch to a spell is by repeating the incantation over and over; saying a spell repeatedly helps to enforce the message, which, in turn, gives it more power each time it is spoken. Generally, a spell is recited no less than three times in a row.

THE WITCH'S MOON–BASED DIET

Some witches like to take complete control of their diets and eat according to the moon's phases. Because so many of us now focus on eating healthily, this practice is becoming more popular with each year. The moon is known to rule tides, which, in turn, affect our body's internal chemistry and our mood swings.

The first twenty-four hours of a moon phase is when the following eating plans should be implemented. Always check with your health-care practitioner before starting any diet.

The Full Moon and the New Moon

The first twenty-four hours of a full or new moon—both are times for new beginnings and cleansing—are the best times for fasting. (Note: Although scientifically a moon phase only lasts an instant because the moon is continuously orbiting the earth, to the naked eye, the new and full phases seem to last about three days—we will consider a phase to be three days for our purposes.) A short spell of fasting is thought to be very good not only for the body but also to bring clarity to the mind and soul. It helps us to focus on what is important and center ourselves into a deeper understanding of spirituality. No solid foods are allowed during this time, only pure water and herbal teas, which help with the detoxification process. Green tea, mint tea, and chamomile tea are perfect for cleansing the body and ridding it of all toxins. Some witches prefer to brew tea from dandelion, lemon, or sage, but any herbal tea will suffice.

For the next two days of the full-moon or new-moon phase, you can happily go back to solid food, but keep your diet rich in vegetables and limit meat. If you must eat meat, eat lean proteins, like fish and chicken.

Otherwise stick to nonmeat sources of protein, like nuts, beans, soy, and quinoa. A cup of herbal tea should be consumed every night before bed and no snacks should be consumed after 6 p.m. This simple detoxification process will help you to shed excess water in the body.

The Waning Crescent Moon
and the Waxing Gibbous Moon

Feasting in time with the phases of the moon can also be beneficial. If you feast during the first twenty-four hours of the waning crescent phase (before a new moon), you can banish bad forces from your life.

Feasting before a waxing gibbous phase (before a full moon) can help you grow and overcome obstacles. The options below list different choices you have for how to eat for the first twenty-four hours of either of these phases of the moon.

- Eat as much as you like during the twenty-four-hour period—no need to feel hungry! If you follow a feast with a fast, both spells become more powerful.

- Eat only in-season fruits, such as apples, oranges, peach, plums, or berries that are easily sourced from your surrounding locality. These can be eaten whole or whizzed up in a juicer to create smoothies.

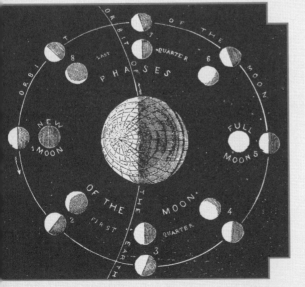

- Eat only boiled vegetables of any kind or salads made with raw vegetables, such as lettuce, cucumber, tomatoes, onions, beets, or potatoes. For each meal, make sure you limit each portion to either all cooked or all uncooked vegetables. For example, don't eat raw cucumbers with the cooked potatoes.

• Eat only cooked (boiled, baked, or grilled) root vegetables, such as pumpkins, gourds, potatoes, carrots, turnips, and parsnips.

• Eat only soups prepared from fresh, seasonal vegetables, using the vegetables to make the soup stocks.

Cooking and preparing your food from scratch using locally sourced and seasonal produce is the best way to ensure a healthy lifestyle. Cooking is an enjoyable part of life that some, although not all, relish. Preparing and cooking food with the right intent will transport magick onto the plate, and that will not only bless the meal but also the people consuming it.

NOTES

NOTES

NOTES

NOTES

NOTES

ABOUT THE AUTHORS

Shawn Robbins

I am an author, a psychic, and a paranormal researcher. The journey that led me to explore the unexplained and the unknown, and took me into the world of medicine, magick, and miracles, began when I was a young girl growing up in Queens, New York. I spent most of my youth reading books on holistic medicine and botanical remedies. Edgar Cayce, who has been called "the father of holistic medicine," became a go-to source for information on healing. But my greatest source of knowledge was my family. My grandparents, immigrants from Russia, and my mother, regaled me with the history and folklore of medicinal plants and herbs, and taught me how to use them in everyday life.

In my early twenties, I met two of the most important people in my life, Bryce Bond, a well-known healer, and Timothy Green Beckley, founder of the New York School of Occult Arts. They helped me realize my childhood dream of helping the ill and infirm, and introduced me to the greatest healers from around the world. I then went on to teach the art of holistic medicine at Tim's school. Still, I sensed that my life was incomplete. Coming from a psychically gifted family, and with my own gift to see into the future and read minds, I knew that there was more in life to learn. Call it fate or kismet, I met the noted parapsychologist Hans Holzer, who helped develop my psychic powers even further, using hypnosis and magnetic energy.

I fervently hope that you will become inspired and empowered to heal yourself and others. Real healing power is within everyone of us. Always remember: Your body is a temple. Nourish it and take care of it; in return, it will take care of you.

I have been practicing witchcraft for more than twenty years. My journey into witchcraft started on my thirteenth birthday when I was given Silver Ravenwolf's *Teen Witch* as a gift. Once I learned that there is a spiritual path connected to the land as well as angelic forces, gods, and a multitude of other spirits, I knew I was home. Everything that both my parents had taught me was found in witchcraft in some form. I had a goddess (Mother Earth) and a god (Father Sky) as well as the creative force (Great Spirit).

Living in Maine today, I am surrounded by nature. My path uses a variety of shamanic techniques, trance work, prayer, meditation, and offerings to connect to the spirits of the land. My witchcraft is wild and free, just like the wilderness of Maine. Over the years I have studied and explored many different styles of witchcraft and paganism. My current path is a mixture of Germanic paganism and traditional witchcraft. Germanic paganism honors the gods of my ancestors (Norse/Anglo-Saxon) and provides a context for honoring my ancestors. Traditional witchcraft allows me to connect with the spirits of the land as well as my ancestors.

I believe strongly that all magickal and spiritual paths have something to teach me. I learned that my path was to help people heal the spirit as well as the mind and body. Today I am a magickal and spiritual herbalist. I craft incenses, powders, tinctures, oils, and ritual baths, and use spiritual and magickal aromatherapy for almost all my magickal practices.

CONTRIBUTORS

Melodie Starr Ball is the creator of the group "Devoted to the Craft" on Facebook.

Derrie P. Carpenter is the creator of the groups "Pagan and Proud" and "Cauldron of Harmony" on Facebook.

Cheryl Croce Culver is the founder of "The Crafty Kitchen WITCH" on Facebook.

Leanna Greenaway is a popular British clairvoyant who has appeared on TV and radio. She is the author or coauthor of numerous books, including *Wiccapedia* (coauthor, from which the Magickal Moon Phases section on pages 9–11 is excerpted) and *Simply Tarot*, and was a columnist for *UK Fate & Fortune Magazine*. She lives in the UK, and you can follow her on her YouTube channel.

Lori Hayes, aka Darklady, is a solitary witch, psychic, medium, and empath. She is the creator of numerous Facebook pages, including "Darklady's Horror Halloween," "Darklady's Spirit Dolls," and "Darklady's Dark Realm."

Connie Lavoie considers herself a creator of "Wiccan/Pagan Group for Beginners" on Facebook and a non-British traditional witch. She was born and raised in Connecticut, resides in southeastern Tennessee, and has been practicing on and off for about fifteen years.

Rachel McGirr is the creator of "The Witches Lair" on Facebook.

Sherry, aka Phoenix Rayn Song, ran "Witches Forum" on Facebook.

Katie Snow is the creator and founder of the group "The Spellery" and Spellery Magazine on Facebook.

PICTURE CREDITS

☀ 2023 ☾

JANUARY 2023
S	M	T	W	T	F	S
1	2	3	4	5	6	7
8	9	10	11	12	13	14
15	16	17	18	19	20	21
22	23	24	25	26	27	28
29	30	31				

FEBRUARY 2023
S	M	T	W	T	F	S
			1	2	3	4
5	6	7	8	9	10	11
12	13	14	15	16	17	18
19	20	21	22	23	24	25
26	27	28				

MARCH 2023
S	M	T	W	T	F	S
			1	2	3	4
5	6	7	8	9	10	11
12	13	14	15	16	17	18
19	20	21	22	23	24	25
26	27	28	29	30	31	

APRIL 2023
S	M	T	W	T	F	S
						1
2	3	4	5	6	7	8
9	10	11	12	13	14	15
16	17	18	19	20	21	22
23	24	25	26	27	28	29
30						

MAY 2023
S	M	T	W	T	F	S
	1	2	3	4	5	6
7	8	9	10	11	12	13
14	15	16	17	18	19	20
21	22	23	24	25	26	27
28	29	30	31			

JUNE 2023
S	M	T	W	T	F	S
				1	2	3
4	5	6	7	8	9	10
11	12	13	14	15	16	17
18	19	20	21	22	23	24
25	26	27	28	29	30	

JULY 2023
S	M	T	W	T	F	S
						1
2	3	4	5	6	7	8
9	10	11	12	13	14	15
16	17	18	19	20	21	22
23	24	25	26	27	28	29
30	31					

AUGUST 2023
S	M	T	W	T	F	S
		1	2	3	4	5
6	7	8	9	10	11	12
13	14	15	16	17	18	19
20	21	22	23	24	25	26
27	28	29	30	31		

SEPTEMBER 2023
S	M	T	W	T	F	S
					1	2
3	4	5	6	7	8	9
10	11	12	13	14	15	16
17	18	19	20	21	22	23
24	25	26	27	28	29	30

OCTOBER 2023
S	M	T	W	T	F	S
1	2	3	4	5	6	7
8	9	10	11	12	13	14
15	16	17	18	19	20	21
22	23	24	25	26	27	28
29	30	31				

NOVEMEBER 2023
S	M	T	W	T	F	S
			1	2	3	4
5	6	7	8	9	10	11
12	13	14	15	16	17	18
19	20	21	22	23	24	25
26	27	28	29	30		

DECEMBER 2023
S	M	T	W	T	F	S
					1	2
3	4	5	6	7	8	9
10	11	12	13	14	15	16
17	18	19	20	21	22	23
24	25	26	27	28	29	30
31						

☀ 2024 ☾

JANUARY 2024
S	M	T	W	T	F	S
	1	2	3	4	5	6
7	8	9	10	11	12	13
14	15	16	17	18	19	20
21	22	23	24	25	26	27
28	29	30	31			

FEBRUARY 2024
S	M	T	W	T	F	S
				1	2	3
4	5	6	7	8	9	10
11	12	13	14	15	16	17
18	19	20	21	22	23	24
25	26	27	28	29		

MARCH 2024
S	M	T	W	T	F	S
					1	2
3	4	5	6	7	8	9
10	11	12	13	14	15	16
17	18	19	20	21	22	23
24	25	26	27	28	29	30
31						

APRIL 2024
S	M	T	W	T	F	S
	1	2	3	4	5	6
7	8	9	10	11	12	13
14	15	16	17	18	19	20
21	22	23	24	25	26	27
28	29	30				

MAY 2024
S	M	T	W	T	F	S
			1	2	3	4
5	6	7	8	9	10	11
12	13	14	15	16	17	18
19	20	21	22	23	24	25
26	27	28	29	30	31	

JUNE 2024
S	M	T	W	T	F	S
						1
2	3	4	5	6	7	8
9	10	11	12	13	14	15
16	17	18	19	20	21	22
23	24	25	26	27	28	29
30						

JULY 2024
S	M	T	W	T	F	S
	1	2	3	4	5	6
7	8	9	10	11	12	13
14	15	16	17	18	19	20
21	22	23	24	25	26	27
28	29	30	31			

AUGUST 2024
S	M	T	W	T	F	S
				1	2	3
4	5	6	7	8	9	10
11	12	13	14	15	16	17
18	19	20	21	22	23	24
25	26	27	28	29	30	31

SEPTEMBER 2024
S	M	T	W	T	F	S
1	2	3	4	5	6	7
8	9	10	11	12	13	14
15	16	17	18	19	20	21
22	23	24	25	26	27	28
29	30					

OCTOBER 2024
S	M	T	W	T	F	S
		1	2	3	4	5
6	7	8	9	10	11	12
13	14	15	16	17	18	19
20	21	22	23	24	25	26
27	28	29	30	31		

NOVEMEBER 2024
S	M	T	W	T	F	S
					1	2
3	4	5	6	7	8	9
10	11	12	13	14	15	16
17	18	19	20	21	22	23
24	25	26	27	28	29	30

DECEMBER 2024
S	M	T	W	T	F	S
1	2	3	4	5	6	7
8	9	10	11	12	13	14
15	16	17	18	19	20	21
22	23	24	25	26	27	28
29	30	31